INSTITUTE OF LEADERSHIP & MANAGEMENT

SUPERSERIES

Improving Efficiency

FOURTH EDITION

Published for the
Institute of Leadership & Management by **Pergamon** *Flexible* **Learning**

AMSTERDAM • BOSTON • HEIDELBERG • LONDON • NEW YORK • OXFORD
PARIS • SAN DIEGO • SAN FRANCISCO • SINGAPORE • SYDNEY • TOKYO

Pergamon Flexible Learning
An imprint of Elsevier
Linacre House, Jordan Hill, Oxford OX2 8DP
200 Wheeler Road, Burlington, MA 01803

First published 1986
Second edition 1991
Third edition 1997
Fourth edition 2003
Reprinted 2004

Permissions may be sought directly from Elsevier's Science and Technology Rights
Department in Oxford, UK: phone: (+44) 1865 843830; fax: (+44) 1865 853333;
e-mail: permissions@elsevier.co.uk.You may also complete your request on-line via
the Elsevier homepage (http://www.elsevier.com), by selecting 'Customer Support'
and then 'Obtaining Permissions'.

British Library Cataloguing in Publication Data
A catalogue record for this book is available from the British Library

ISBN 0 7506 5871 1

For information on Pergamon Flexible Learning
visit our website at www.bh.com/pergamonfl

Institute of Leadership & Management
registered office
1 Giltspur Street
London
EC1A 9DD
Telephone 020 7294 3053
www.i-l-m.com
ILM is part of the City & Guilds Group

The views expressed in this work are those of the authors and do
not necessarily reflect those of the Institute of Leadership &
Management or of the publisher

Authors: Joe Johnson and Deirdre Thackray
Editor: Eileen Cadman
Editorial management: Genesys, www.genesys-consultants.com
Based on previous material by Joe Johnson
Composition by Genesis Typesetting Limited, Rochester, Kent
Printed and bound in Great Britain by MPG Books, Bodmin

Contents

Contents

Workbook introduction

1 ILM Super Series study links

This workbook addresses the issues of *Improving Efficiency*. Should you wish to extend your study to other Super Series workbooks covering related or different subject areas, you will find a comprehensive list at the back of this book.

2 Links to ILM Qualifications

This workbook relates to the following learning outcomes in segments from the ILM Level 3 Introductory Certificate in First Line Management and the Level 3 Certificate in First Line Management.

C1.6   Effectiveness and Efficiency
1. Understand the terms effectiveness and efficiency and recognise the difference
2. Recognise the link between effectiveness and achievement of results
3. Recognise the link between efficiency and cost/performance standards
4. Use processes which balance effectiveness and efficiency
5. Assess extent of achievement of objectives.

C6.5 People as a Resource
1 Plan the activities of workteam members to achieve organizational objectives
2 Organize people's work activities in an efficient and effective manner
3 Identify staffing needs and make recommendations on staffing levels.

C6.6 Equipment
1 Understand the need for effective and efficient use of equipment
2 Monitor and control the use of equipment in own work area
3 Plan to maintain equipment in a safe, efficient and effective manner.

C6.8 Minimising Waste
1 Identify areas of potential physical waste – including misuse, extravagance, scrap, rework, shrinkage or others as appropriate
2 Use appropriate measurement techniques to quantify waste
3 Draw up, implement and review action plans to reduce waste.

3 Links to S/NVQs in Management

This workbook relates to the following elements of the Management Standards which are used in S/NVQs in Management, as well as a range of other S/NVQs.

B1.1 Make recommendations for the use of resources
B1.2 Contribute to the control of resources.

It is designed to help you demonstrate the following Personal Competences:

- communicating
- focusing on results
- thinking and taking decisions

4 Workbook objectives

In 1995 Sir John Harvey-Jones wrote:

> We talk continuously about the need to improve our productivity and, God knows, it is a dire need: yet we appear to accept with equanimity that in the world of work we are achieving less than half our capacity. Luckily for us few other countries do much better, but the potential for improvement is so vast that it is incomprehensible that we do not debate, study and struggle to do better.
> (Source: John Harvey-Jones (1995) *All Together Now*, Mandarin.)

What was true in 1995 is, sadly, still true today. We still have a long way to go before we can say that our businesses run as efficiently as they might.

However, by deciding to study this workbook you have taken the first step towards addressing the problem of managing your organization's resources in an efficient and effective manner so that costs are reduced and waste is minimized.

There are four sessions. Sessions A and C can be summarized very concisely, as follows:

> Work is about converting resources into outputs. These resources are capital, materials, information, energy, equipment, time, finance and people. It is in the optimum management of resources that efficiency is achieved. The manager desiring improvements in efficiency must therefore identify the resources at his or her command, and find ways of getting the best from them.

Although Session B is not central to this theme, it is very relevant, and you should find it informative. It deals with ways of measuring and analysing work processes: productivity, work study and some of the latest thinking about how to improve the efficiency of organizations.

A story which illustrates the distinction between efficiency and effectiveness is that of a surgeon who was said to have improved his efficiency by completing more operations in a day, only to reduce his effectiveness as all his patients died.

All organizations would like their employees to be more efficient because **efficiency** is normally equated with profitability. One way of expressing efficiency is as an equation: what you get out divided by what you put in:

$$\frac{\text{what you get out}}{\text{what you put in}}$$

Effectiveness, on the other hand, has to do with how good you are at achieving what you set out to achieve.

Session D highlights the risk to profitability caused by failure to control waste. You are shown how to identify sources of waste in your work processes, and develop an action plan to reduce it.

One misplaced fear is that increased efficiency leads to job losses. The argument is that fewer people will be needed to perform the same tasks. In fact, the opposite is generally true. When efficiency goes up, an organization becomes more prosperous, is able to expand its sphere of activities, and so more people are likely to be needed.

4.1 Objectives

When you have completed this workbook you will be better able to:

- recognize what efficiency means in the context of your workplace
- identify and use some method study techniques to help you improve efficiency and effectiveness
- plan for the best use of resources, including people, assigned to you
- contribute effectively to the control of your organization's resources
- carry out a review of actual and potential waste generation points and take action to reduce waste accordingly
- play your part in helping to improve the efficiency of your work team and your organization.

5 Activity planner

The following activities require some planning so you may want to look at these now.

- Activity 21 on page 51 starts the process of creating a structured approach to increasing efficiency by finding ways to advance the potential of your team. This is continued in Activity 27 on page 59.
- Activity 22 on page 52 helps you to make optimum use of your workspace. You might like to start making a note of problems and requirements now. This is continued in Activity 28 on page 60.

- Activity 23 on page 53 will provide you with the basis of a structured approach to increased efficiency in the use of machinery and equipment. This is continued in Activity 29.
- Activity 24 on page 54 provides the basis of a structured approach to increased efficiency in the use of materials. This is continued in Activity 30 on page 62.
- Activity 26 on page 56 provides the basis of a structured approach to improving the use you make of sources of information. This is continued in Activity 32 on page 64.
- Activity 31 on page 63 provides the basis for a structured approach to making better use of energy in the workplace.
- Activity 33 on page 71 asks you to look at the legislation and regulations that apply to waste control in your work area.
- Activity 37 on page 76 requires you to design and distribute a questionnaire.

Some or all of these Activities may provide the basis of evidence for your S/NVQ portfolio. All Portfolio Activities and the Work-based assignment are signposted with this icon.

The icon states the elements to which the Portfolio Activities and Work-based assignment relate.

The Work-based assignment (on page 92) asks you to develop one pair of these Activities into a complete plan for improving efficiency with respect to one resource at your command. This could also be used to form the basis for your portfolio of evidence. You may want to prepare for it in advance.

Session A
Background to efficiency

1 Introduction

One of the great gurus of management theory, Peter Drucker, used to say that the only thing that differentiates one business from another is the quality of its management. And the only way to measure that quality is through a measurement of productivity that shows how well resources are utilised and how much they yield. (Peter F Drucker, *The Practice of Management.*[1])

Managers need to have many qualities, including: industry, honesty, self-confidence, a sense of fairness, moral courage, consistency, audacity. Commendable as these attributes are, they are very difficult to measure, and they don't **necessarily** lead to good results for the organization. Efficiency (or productivity), on the other hand, can usually be calculated, and the efficient manager is recognized as a successful manager.

Taking another view, the work managers do can be said to consist of:

- achieving desired results by giving direction to others
- balancing efficiency and effectiveness
- getting the most from limited resources.

The last two of these are the subjects of this workbook.

This session aims to help you get a good understanding of efficiency and effectiveness at work.

---

[1] Paperback edition (1989), page 68, Butterworth-Heinemann.

2 Work organizations

It can be useful to classify work organizations into four groups or sectors. We have the:

- **manufacturing sector**, where goods are produced
- **transport sector**, in which people or goods are transferred
- **supply sector**, which supplies goods it does not manufacture
- **service sector**, where services, rather than physical goods, are passed to the customer.

Activity 1

2 mins

Which sector or sectors do your employers fall into?

_____

_____

Most organizations are not difficult to categorize. All manufacturers, of whatever commodity, are obviously in the first group. Apart from industrial companies, manufacturing includes agriculture, the construction industry, and the energy producers, i.e. generators of electricity and manufacturers of gas and oil products.

Airlines, bus companies and freight companies are all in the transportation business. Shops, distributors, car dealers and so on fall into the supply sector. The service sector includes such organizations as hairdressers, building societies, restaurants, etc.

Of course, some companies, especially the larger corporations, can claim to be represented in more than one sector. Marks and Spencer plc, for example, supplies clothes and food, and offers financial services. The Virgin group's enterprises include shops (supply), radio broadcasting (service), and an airline (transport). Also, some industries really straddle two sectors: holiday travel companies are not simply in the business of transporting people; their main aim is to offer a service.

Which of these four sectors is the largest?

In many countries, including the UK, the service sector has long since supplanted manufacturing as the largest group, with that trend likely to continue.

You may read or hear people lamenting the 'decline of our great manufacturing industries'. In the United States, the same sentiments are often expressed. These complaints may be justified in the sense that those countries with a strong manufacturing base have traditionally been among the richest. However, there are many who argue that this is less true today. Britain may make fewer cars and tractors than it used to, but it exports a vast range of services which earn a great deal of money and prestige.

Whatever you think about this, you will perhaps agree that it is silly to suggest that one work sector is somehow more 'worthy' than another. Real work is done in all organizations.

But we are getting away from our subject. Let's now turn to the question of what work itself consists of.

3 Work as a transforming process

When we do work on something, we change it in some way. A wood-turner takes a piece of wood and (literally) turns it into a chair leg; a skilled gardener can transform a plot of rough ground into a delight to the eye by filling it with flowers and shrubs; a builder changes bricks and mortar into houses. Another way of putting it is to say that all work is a **transforming** process.

Thus we can say that work organizations of all kinds carry out transformations. In its simplest form, the work process is shown by the following diagram:

| Inputs | → | Transformations | → | Outputs |

Transformations consist of one or more of three types:

- improving
- caretaking
- transferring.

The simplest examples to identify are those in the manufacturing sector. A power station has inputs of water plus coal, oil or nuclear fuel, and it 'improves' these inputs first to steam and then to electricity, its final output. Textile mills transform fibres into cloth. To 'improve' is another way of saying 'add value to'.

The inputs and outputs of a school happen to be the same: children. The transformations taking place here are those of caretaking – safeguarding through a period of time, and improving – increasing the children's knowledge and understanding.

What about transferring? We can say that a taxi company 'transforms' people by transferring them to their desired destination, while taking care of them during the journey. A waste disposal company is also in the business of transferring and caretaking.

Activity 2

4 mins

Jot down the inputs, transformation processes and outputs of your own organization (or, if there are many, **three** or **four** of them).

Inputs	Transformation type	Outputs
_____	_____	_____
_____	_____	_____
_____	_____	_____
_____	_____	_____

In case you had difficulty with this, here are a few more examples.

An airline transfers people from one place to another (movement in space), while taking care of them through time, and (conceivably) 'improving' them by making them more rested, or better fed.

A chiropodist improves people by attending to their feet. Financial advisers have as their inputs the financial affairs of their clients, which they aim to improve by proposing sound investments. A baker converts flour and yeast into bread and cakes. Farmers take as inputs seeds, soil and fertilizers in order to produce outputs of crops. The inputs of beauticians could be said to be the faces and bodies of their customers, which they try to improve by making them more beautiful.

EXTENSION 1
Introduction to Operations Management, John Naylor. Most of the topics covered in this workbook are typically included under the general topic area of **operations management**.

Operations management is defined in the book of the same name by John Naylor as follows:

> Operations management is concerned with creating, operating and controlling a transformation system which takes inputs of a variety of resources and produces outputs of goods and services which are needed by customers.

4 Introduction to resources

The inputs to work processes are called **resources**, which can be classified in at least three ways. You may see resources separated into:

- **m**oney
- **m**anpower
- **m**achines and
- **m**aterials

– the four Ms.

A second classification is 'land, capital and labour'. Here, land is the term used to describe all natural resources, including water, airspace and raw materials. Capital is all non-human, non-natural resources, and labour is the term used for human resources.

However, the most usual way of categorizing resources, and the one we will use, is:

- people
- capital
- materials
- information.

Let's look at what we mean by these four groups.

■ **People** (also called **labour**): those who run the organization, and work in it

It should be said from the start that many object to applying the word 'resource' to people.

It does seem strange and unfeeling to think of people as a resource. We do this simply for convenience. But it is important to remember, when bracketing employees alongside capital, materials and information, that:

people are the most precious, most flexible and most necessary of all the resources of an organization.

Without people to organize and direct the work, nothing worthwhile can be achieved, even in those workplaces where there is a high level of automation.

Getting the best from people, whether or not you classify them as a resource, is the most challenging aspect of a manager's job.

■ **Capital**: equipment, machinery, finance, land, buildings and goodwill

We define capital as the permanent or semi-permanent assets of the organization, apart from people, which are needed to enable goods and services to be produced.

Deciding how equipment, finance, land, buildings and goodwill can be used to best effect occupies much of the time and efforts of management.

■ **Materials**: raw materials and components, which are converted or consumed by the process, together with the energy consumed

These are the direct inputs: the ingredients which are used up in producing the goods or services that are the outputs of an organization.

Frequently, this is the group of resources where the most waste occurs, and which consequently has the greatest potential for savings and improved efficiency.

■ **Information**: a vital resource, which includes the know-how to do the work, knowledge of competitors and markets, and so on

No work can be done without intelligence. Often, it is the best informed managers who are the most effective and efficient.

Time is sometimes listed as a separate resource, and is certainly a constraining factor in all human endeavour.

It is difficult to think of an organization which can operate without every one of these resources. Our model can therefore be modified to:

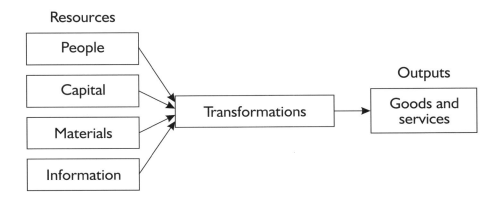

Resources

| People |
| Capital |
| Materials |
| Information |

Transformations

Outputs

| Goods and services |

Activity 3

3 mins

Now think about your own organization again, and list a few of its resources as people, capital, materials and information. Jot down just **three** examples of each type.

People: _____

Capital: _____

Materials: _____

Information: _____

Answers to this Activity can be found on pages 105–06.

We need to go on to discuss resources in more detail, but before doing that, we should return to our main theme: efficiency and effectiveness.

5 Efficiency

By defining exactly what we mean by efficiency and effectiveness, we will have a better idea of how resources can be used efficiently and effectively.

Activity 4

How would you define the word 'efficiency'?

_____

_____

_____

There are several ways to express what efficiency means; compare your answer with the following. Efficiency has been defined as:

- 'a measure of how well resources are transformed into outputs'
- 'working well with little waste'
- 'getting the most out of what you put in'
- 'the production of the maximum result from the minimum effort'
- 'the best use of resources to achieve production of goods or services'.

The last definition is the one most meaningful in the context of this workbook. To be efficient, we must make the best use of resources, that is, we have to find ways of utilizing resources to produce the goods or services we want, with the minimum of waste. To repeat the definition:

Efficiency means making the best use of resources in achieving production of goods or services.

The main purpose of the workbook is to investigate ways in which this can be done. Relevant activities in achieving efficiency at work are likely to include:

- developing existing resources
- reducing the amount or cost of resources
- utilizing existing resources in the best way
- finding better resources than the ones we have
- minimizing waste.

5.1 Why is efficiency important?

It may seem obvious to say that all organizations want to be more efficient. But why? What is the effect of increased efficiency? So far as any commercial company is concerned, the answer can be summed up in the following diagram:

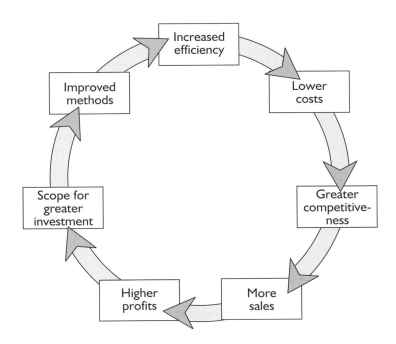

As you can see, the effects are self-regenerating. As efficiency increases, so costs go down, and the organization has leeway to reduce prices, resulting in enhanced competitiveness. This leads to higher sales and profits, and opens the way for the organization to invest in even better methods of production. Efficiency can then be raised even more, and the cycle continues.

5.2 Efficiency and control

At each point of the cycle there must be an element of control. Without control it will be difficult to gauge how efficient the organization is becoming, or where changes in performance are proving as efficient as required. All managers will recognize that their role includes a degree of control, particularly in relation to the use of the organization's resources.

Control will result in:

■ planning processes which are more likely to succeed
■ achievement of objectives

- identification and use of resources which are of the correct quality and quantity
- ability to take appropriate corrective action – less reactive, more proactive response to problems
- improved forecasting and estimating
- thorough assessment of performance, enabling constructive feedback and improved staff performance overall.

Activity 5 · 5mins

What day-to-day methods of control do you use, and how do they contribute to efficient working?

_____

_____

_____

Methods and types of control will vary between organizations, but essentially they will have a similar purpose – to ensure that working practices result in the organization achieving its objectives and enhancing its performance.

5.3 Balancing efficiency with effectiveness

Peter Drucker described efficiency as 'doing things right', and effectiveness as 'doing the right things'.

Effectiveness has also been defined as:

- 'an assessment of how far a stated objective is achieved'
- 'being concerned with the achievement of set organizational goals or objectives'.

There is an important distinction between efficiency and effectiveness. It is perfectly possible to be efficient and yet ineffective, as you read in the Workbook introduction. The jeweller who saves on materials while producing brooches that no one wants to wear can hardly claim to have attained her objectives.

Objectives are the prime driver in terms of effectiveness and efficiency. It will always be possible for someone to achieve objectives where every conceivable resource is made available. In this case the jeweller can be argued to have been effective – she achieved her objective. However this is not efficient because, as we have already learned, **efficiency means making the best use of resources.**

Balancing effectiveness and efficiency is part of the managerial role, and will require you as a manager in using the most appropriate methods and types of control available to you.

It is most likely that the objectives of your organization will include reference to its customers – the people to which it provides goods and services.

Workteam objectives are typically expanded versions of the following:

> 'We aim to provide a first class service (or high quality goods) to our customers, in an efficient manner.'

Your customers may be another team, or they may be the customers of the organization itself.

All commercial enterprises must ultimately direct their activities towards satisfying their customers. Even non-commercial organizations, such as charities and schools, can be said to have customers. So our earlier model of work organizations should be modified just once more to give:

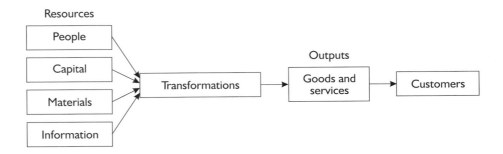

Work organizations transform resources (capital, materials and information, with the help of people) into goods and services, which are provided to their customers.

This model can help us identify sources of inefficiency and ineffectiveness.

Activity 6

Examine the *Resources:Transformations:Outputs:Customers* model above.

Try to identify two potential examples of **inefficiency.** Describe where within the model they might occur, and what the impact might be at later stages. One example might be having the wrong quality of materials, which will result in customer dissatisfaction later in the model.

_____

_____

Now, try to identify two potential examples of **ineffectiveness**. Again, describe where within the model they might occur, and what the impact might be at later stages. You could say, for example, producing a product which has no customers willing to buy it.

_____

_____

The answer to this question can be found on page 106

Here are some further examples of inefficiency and ineffectiveness.

A manicurist could be inefficient by wasting materials, turning up late for appointments, and so on. Ineffectiveness might presumably be accomplished by breaking the clients' nails.

If a school canteen were to spoil food, it would be less than fully efficient. But if it were to cook insufficient meals for the number of children to be served, so that some went hungry, it would be less than fully effective.

In a similar way, a bricklayer who damaged new bricks might be called inefficient. Building a crooked wall, though, should cause the bricklayer to be labelled both ineffective (in not achieving the aim of building a straight wall), *and* inefficient (in thereby causing the wall to have to be built again).

If we want to be efficient and effective, we have to find ways of doing the opposite kinds of things from those mentioned above.

The concept of effectiveness is relevant to all jobs, and efficiency is relevant to nearly all, no matter what products or services are provided by the organization.

6 Quality

There's one other very relevant topic worth taking a look at before getting back to the subject of resources, and that is 'quality'.

Activity 7

4 mins

How would you define 'high quality'? Try to sum up the meaning of these words in a couple of sentences. You could, for example, start by thinking about what you mean by high quality as a customer, when you buy something in a shop.

_____

_____

_____

_____

You might say that high quality means:

- getting the kind of products and services that you want
- conforming to a high standard
- the best there is
- excellence.

These are all correct, so far as they go.

When we want to buy something – whether it is food, clothing, luxury items or any other product – we usually have a good deal of choice. There may be a number of different shops and outlets selling goods made by a number of different manufacturers.

Because of all this choice, the goods and services which best meet the needs of customers will sell well. The goods and services which fail to provide customers with what they want will not sell so well – or may not sell at all.

Quality is in fact concerned with **every** aspect of a product.

Quality can be defined as all the features and characteristics of a product or service which affect its ability to satisfy the needs of customers and users.

This definition provides a clue to the link between efficiency, effectiveness and quality. We have already agreed that effectiveness means the achievement of objectives, and that the objectives of all commercial organizations are inevitably linked to satisfying customers.

It is the most effective organizations that are best able to achieve high standards of quality, by delivering the products and services that their customers want. And it is the most efficient ones that are able to survive and prosper in competitive markets.

We will not dwell further on quality in this workbook. You will find more information on this subject in *Achieving Quality* in this series.

However, before we move on, it is worth mentioning 'the **five rights of customers**'. These are the aspects of quality that every customer has a right to expect. They are:

- the right product or service
- of the right quality
- at the right time
- in the right place
- at the right price.

Only when a commercial organization consistently delivers products or services which meet these expectations can it say that it is being fully effective in its objectives in satisfying its customers.

In the next five sections, we return to the subject of resources.

7 People as a resource

On page 5 we listed the resources which are inputs to the work process. They are:

- people
- capital
- materials
- information.

Let's look at people first.

Activity 8 · 15 mins

Read the following statements carefully, and comment upon them. In each case, tick the appropriate box to indicate whether you think it is, in your experience, 'accurate', 'partially accurate' or 'inaccurate'. Then write a sentence or two explaining the reason for your choice. Think about your own organization as you answer.

	Accurate	Partially accurate	Inaccurate

I think the employees of an organization are typically:

a an underdeveloped resource; ☐ ☐ ☐

because _____

_____

b more caring about, and interested in, their work than most employers recognize; ☐ ☐ ☐

because _____

_____

c an undervalued resource; ☐ ☐ ☐

because _____

_____

d treated as if they could easily be replaced; ☐ ☐ ☐

because _____

_____

e less efficient or reliable than machines; ☐ ☐ ☐

because _____

_____

f the most adaptable, precious and potentially useful resource the organization has. ☐ ☐ ☐

because _____

Your views on these statements are as valid as the next person's. There are no right or wrong answers. Compare your response with the following points.

a There seems to be little doubt that, in many organizations, people are an underdeveloped resource. You may feel that you, or other members of your team, are not being given the opportunities to use your abilities to the full. Most employers create and define jobs, and then try to find the people to fill them. This is inevitably a difficult matching process. While many employees find themselves capable of fulfilling their assigned roles, they may in truth not feel well suited to the job they are made to do.

In smaller organizations, and in some enlightened larger ones, the task may be moulded to the individual, rather than the other way round. The question changes from one of 'What should the person in this job be doing?' to 'What are we as individuals capable of, and how can our combined skills be used to achieve our objectives?' This approach gives people greater scope for self-expression and development.

The subject of getting the best from people is taken up again in Session C.

b A related question is that of whether employees are more caring about, and interested in, their work than most employers recognize. Again, your response will reflect your experience and point of view; it depends on the people, and on the employer. Most people do care about their jobs, and would be willing to contribute more, given some encouragement.

c,d Are employees an undervalued resource? This is perhaps a more debatable point. If you decided that this statement is accurate, it may be that you feel undervalued yourself, or have seen organizations or executives who treat their workers with scant regard.

Certainly, when so many people have lost their jobs in recent years (said to be over 5 million employees in the 1990s in the UK alone), an unbiased observer might think that employees are often treated as if they were expendable. 'Cost cutting' and 'improvements in efficiency' can sometimes seem to be an excuse for organizations to lay off staff.

e Are people less efficient or less reliable than machines? Perhaps you will agree that there is some truth in this. When it comes to performing routine tasks repetitively, there is no contest: automated processes win easily. But the time has not yet come when machines can truly 'think'. We have not yet seen a factory where the intelligence and thinking efficiency of people is not needed. (However, who can say this will never happen?)

People at work do get replaced by machines, and the justification is usually an economic one. However, you don't *necessarily* increase efficiency simply by introducing more equipment; every case has to be considered on its merits.

f   You will perhaps agree that this last statement is accurate. Employees are the most adaptable, precious and potentially useful resource the organization has.

As we will discuss later in the workbook, an important approach to achieving improvements in efficiency is to find ways of getting the best from your team.

8 Capital as a resource

8.1 Land and buildings

The land and buildings of an organization, assuming they are owned outright, are usually among its most valuable assets. It goes without saying, therefore, that they should be used efficiently and effectively.

Activity 9   3 mins

What do you think is entailed in making effective and efficient use of land and buildings? Try to list **two** things.

_____

_____

_____

Some points you may have mentioned are that buildings and land should be:

- maintained properly, so that they retain their value
- allocated between people, sections and departments so that each group has the right amount of space and facilities, in the right location

■ developed to their full potential; for example, an old building may need to be demolished and replaced (subject to current planning regulations) if it no longer serves the needs of the organization adequately.

8.2 Finance

By finance, we mean funds (i.e. available money) or the provision of funds. Of course, buildings, land and other resources are valuable, but they would first have to be sold before they could be used to purchase other things.

> Budgets are itemized summaries of expected income and expenditure over a period.

Unless you work in the finance department of your organization, the primary way in which you help to control finance will probably be through **budgets**.

In Session C, we will briefly discuss ways in which first line managers can contribute to the efficient use of finance. In the meantime, you might like to start giving some thought to the following questions. You may not feel you can write down answers straight away; if you can't, keep the questions in mind as you go about your work in the next few days.

Activity 10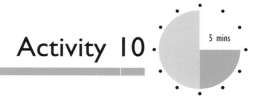

5 mins

How could you keep the finance you are responsible for under better control?

_____

_____

_____

What further information, if any, would help you do this?

_____

_____

_____

18.3 Equipment

Equipment and machinery are the tools of work, and may include items as diverse as screwdrivers, computers, knitting needles, ovens, sewing machines and welding gear. Often, machinery is both expensive and complicated, and requires a good deal of understanding if it is to be used efficiently. As with other assets, a proper schedule of maintenance is usually necessary.

The efficient use of equipment is covered in more detail in Session C.

8.4 Goodwill

The capital of an organization includes intangible items that are sometimes difficult to put a value on. Probably the most important of these is **goodwill**.

Activity 11   3 mins

Explain briefly what you understand by the term 'goodwill'.

_____

_____

_____

How might goodwill be lost, and what will be the effects if it is lost?

_____

_____

_____

As you might have said, the goodwill of an organization is the value of how it is seen by others – its good reputation. Goodwill has real worth, which can be realized when the organization is sold.

Goodwill may be lost by, for example:

- delivering poor quality goods or services to customers
- dealing with customers in an high-handed fashion
- failing to address complaints or concerns expressed by members of the public
- having poor relations with the press
- having an uncaring attitude to the environment.

In the case of commercial companies, the effects of lost goodwill are, sooner or later, loss of profits resulting from lost sales.

Loss of goodwill comes about through ineffectiveness or inefficiency, and leads to reduced profits.

9 Materials as a resource

Material resources are those things consumed (energy and consumable items) or converted (raw materials and components) during the work process.

For example, hospitals consume hypodermic needles, drugs, bandages, and blood and convert sick people to well ones; printers consume ink and convert blank paper to printed copy; poachers consume shot-gun pellets and convert live animals to dead ones; laundries consume washing powder and water and convert dirty washing to clean.

If you can save on materials you will automatically become more efficient.

Activity 12

2 mins

From your own work area give two examples each of:

■ consumed material resources
■ converted material resources

_____

_____

_____

_____

10 Information as a resource

Although people may complain that there is ineffective or inefficient communication within their organization this is rarely because there is insufficient information. Generally speaking there is more than enough information made available to us every day. We are bombarded with images, ideas, suggestions and news.

For information to be a valid and reliable resource it should be:

■ accurate and complete
■ sufficient and available at a time when it can support decision-making and problem-solving processes
■ formatted in a way which suits the needs of the recipient, for example paper-based or electronic
■ easy to access and retrieve.

Activity 13

15 mins

Identify three items of information which are essential to the work processes in your area of responsibility. For each of these briefly explain:

- where/who it comes from
- how you receive the information
- what you use it for
- any problems you have experienced in relation to this information (consider the list above) and possible ways of solving them.

1 _____

   _____

   _____

   _____

2 _____

   _____

   _____

   _____

3 _____

   _____

   _____

   _____

This Activity should have helped you to realise how important information is in your every day working life. It should also have enabled you to identify problem areas and possible solutions.

11 Time as a resource

Time is not always regarded as a separate resource because it is assumed to be part of the use of people. It is so important, however, that it is worth separate consideration here.

Sometimes, saving time can lead directly to increased efficiency. The rule is simple and fairly obvious: if you can perform a task more quickly **without increasing your use of other resources**, then you have improved efficiency. If this is not the case, then the saving in time must be balanced against any extra costs involved.

Self-assessment 1

10 mins

1   Complete the following diagram, by writing in the correct words:

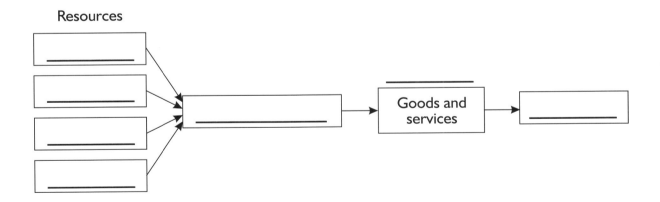

Resources

Goods and services

2 Place the following types of work organization in the most appropriate cells in the table:

a A UK regional electricity company.
b A UK water company.
c A hairdresser.
d A hardware shop.
e A residential school.
f A farm.

Transformation type	Sector			
	Manufacturing	Transport	Supply	Service
Improving				
Caretaking				
Transferring				

3 Complete the following statements by replacing the blanks with suitable words:

a _____ means making the best use of _____, to achieve production of goods or _____.

b Work organizations _____ resources (capital, materials and _____, with the help of _____) into goods and services, which are provided to their _____.

c _____ can be defined as all the _____ and character-istics of a product or service that affect its ability to _____ the needs of customers and _____.

d For information to be valid and reliable it must be _____ and complete.

4 Suggest two benefits to an organization tht can arise as the result of control.

Answers to these questions can be found on pages 101–3.

12 Summary

- Work organizations can be categorized into four sectors: manufacturing; transport; supply; service.

- Work can be described as a transforming process; transformations may consist of improving, caretaking or transferring.

- Resources are the inputs to the work process, and may be listed as people, capital, materials and information.

- Efficiency means making the best use of resources, to achieve production of goods or services.

- Effectiveness is concerned with the achievement of organizational goals or objectives.

- It is the most effective organizations who are best able to achieve high standards of quality, by delivering the products and services that their customers want. And it is the most efficient ones who are able to survive and prosper in competitive markets.

- People are the most adaptable, precious and potentially useful resource an organization has.

- The land and buildings of an organization, assuming they are owned outright, are usually among its most valuable assets, and therefore should be used efficiently and effectively.

- By finance, we mean funds (i.e. available money) or the provision of funds.

- Often, equipment is both expensive and complicated, and requires a good deal of understanding.

- The goodwill of an organization can be described as the value of how it is seen by others. It is lost through inefficiency or ineffectiveness.

- If you can save on materials, you will automatically become more efficient.

- Materials come in two forms: those that are consumed and those that are converted.

- Every manager can contribute to energy savings.

- Information must be valid and reliable if it is to be a useful resource.

- If you can perform a task quicker without increasing your use of other resources, then you will have improved efficiency.

Session B
Productivity and work study

1 Introduction

We know what efficiency is, but how can we measure it? How will we recognize it when we see it?

If possible, it would be useful to express efficiency in numerical terms, so that we have a sound basis for comparison. And if we were able to divide work activities into small elements, we could set a standard time for performing each one, and calculate how long a task 'should' take, compared with what it does take.

The techniques described in this session attempt to do these things. Productivity reduces efficiency to a simple ratio. Method study is the breaking down of tasks into individual elements, and then analysing them. Work measurement uses techniques to determine how long a qualified worker takes to do a specified job to a defined level of performance.

2 Productivity

If you recall, our definition of efficiency was as follows.

Efficiency means making the best use of resources to achieve production of goods or services.

In its simplest form, efficiency can be expressed as a ratio of what we get out for what we put in, i.e.:

$$\frac{\text{output}}{\text{input}}$$

This ratio is referred to as **productivity**, and can be applied at a national as well as organizational level.

Let's put some numbers into this ratio. Say the inputs – the resources used – for a certain job cost £1000 and the output was valued at £2000.

Then the input:output ratio would be:

$$\frac{2000}{1000}$$

We can simplify this to:

$$\frac{2}{1}$$

This is known as the job's productivity ratio.

If we wanted to get an increase in productivity we could either **increase** the output for the same input or **decrease** the input for the same output. If for example we could increase the output value from £2000 to £3000, the ratio would become:

$$\frac{3}{1}$$

On the other hand, if the resource input costs fell from £1000 to £500 (with the output still valued at £2000), the ratio would become:

$$\frac{2}{0.5} \quad \text{or} \quad \frac{4}{1}$$

In other words:

Productivity rises if the output is increased without increasing the input, or if the output stays the same but the input is decreased.

2.1 Company productivity ratios

Some examples of productivity ratios used in organizations are:

(a)
$$\frac{\text{Sales}}{\text{Labour hours}}$$

(b)
$$\frac{\text{Sales}}{\text{Pay}}$$

(c)
$$\frac{\text{Value of shipments}}{\text{Labour and materials}}$$

(d)
$$\frac{\text{Value of production}}{\text{Cost of labour + materials + capital + overheads}}$$

Activity 14

3 mins

Consider the following example.

Suppose you own a vineyard, and have the aim of getting rich by making lots of high quality wine. You could measure your productivity as:

1
$$\frac{\text{Number of bottles of wine produced}}{\text{Number of hectares of vineyard}}$$

2
$$\frac{\text{Value of wine produced}}{\text{Labour costs}}$$

3
$$\frac{\text{Value of wine produced}}{\text{Cost of all resources used}}$$

(a) Which ratio would give you the best overall indication of efficiency? Tick your answer.

1 ☐   2 ☐   3 ☐

(b) Are all these ratios true measures of efficiency? Circle your answer.

Yes/No

Explain your answer to question (b):

_____

_____

Perhaps you will agree that ratio 3 is the best overall indication of efficiency. But what about the answer to (b)?

Suppose now that in one year in your vineyard you have a good crop of grapes, but make a mistake and pick them at the wrong time. You would probably still be able to make large quantities of wine, but it wouldn't be very good. You might have to sell the wine at a price that barely made you a profit.

If you used ratio 1, you could claim that your productivity was high, in terms of yield per hectare. This is a perfectly valid measure of productivity, and is the kind of figure used to compare the output of one vineyard with another. However, if you picked your crop at the wrong time you can hardly profess to have made 'the best use of resources', so your efficiency cannot be said to be high. (Incidentally, your effectiveness would not be very good, either, as you will have failed in your aims.)

Often, ratios and other statistical information can be misleading, and it is important to think carefully about what the figures really mean. In the above case, the key difference was that ratio 1 was in terms of the number of bottles, not the wine's value. In commercial organizations, it is sensible to assess overall productivity as a ratio of money: cost and value.

3 Cost benefit analysis

To achieve efficient and effective working we have already established that there will be associated costs. We have also considered the different types of resource needed to support an organization's activity. Associated with each of the four types of resource – people, capital, materials, information – there are bound to be costs. Costs can fall into two types:

- quantitative
- qualitative.

'Quantitative' is the term used when costs are described in numerical terms or units. For example, if we state that the cost of an item was £23, we are using the quantitative description. 'Qualitative' is the term used when costs are set out in broad descriptive or less tangible terms. For example, if we state that the cost to the business was a decrease in morale, we are using the qualitative description, i.e. it is difficult to attribute numerical terms in this instance, but there is a cost nonetheless.

The same terms and terminology can be attributed to benefits.

We can use cost benefit analysis methodology in a range of instances, for example:

■ when purchasing a new piece of equipment
■ when introducing new work schedules
■ when changing staff rostering systems.

A cost benefit analysis is likely to result in some form of business case in order to justify a decision (positive or negative) that is being made. This case may be made formally in report format, in a presentation, or simply during discussions with others within the organisation.

3.1 Costs

EXTENSION 3
For more detail on managing costs, see *Operations Management* by Howard Barnett.

To justify the purchase of a new piece of equipment, or any form of change, it is generally accepted that the total benefits will exceed the total costs.

If, for example, you have been asked to conduct a cost benefit analysis in relation to the potential purchase of a new piece of capital equipment, costs will possibly include:

1 The investigation of possible suppliers, including calls, travel and time.

2 The actual purchase (or lease if this is an option).

3 Installation and commissioning of the equipment.

4 Delivery and location on-site.

5 Time spent training staff on how to use.

6 Duplicate costs incurred in running of existing equipment during phasing-in stage.

7 Down time if old equipment is to be removed before installation of new.

8 Staff down time while waiting for installation.

9 Potential opportunity costs where, if the money is spent on one thing, the opportunity is lost for spending it on something else.

Activity 15

Which of the above costs are quantitative and which are qualitative?

Quantitative:

_____

_____

_____

Qualitative:

_____

_____

_____

The answers to this question can be found on page 106.

3.2 Benefits

Benefits are always likely to have associated timescales; they may be immediate benefits or they may become apparent in the short, medium or long term.

Benefits may be:

- actual reduction in costs
- saving time, for example where old equipment requires a high level of maintenance and/or repair
- saving physical effort, for example where new equipment is designed in a way which reduces the physical energy required to operate more efficiently and effectively
- transfer of labour to other areas
- more skilled workforce that can adapt more readily to future technological advances.

These benefits will be in quantitative and qualitative terms, and it may not be easy to specify the actual long-term benefits to the business as a whole, particularly where they are clearly qualitative benefits.

The remainder of this session will explore the examination of work methods, or work study, as it is more commonly known. Cost benefit analysis will always be important here, as it will be necessary to decide where changes in work methods are required, and what the costs and benefits of these changes might be.

4 Work study

4.1 Introduction to work study

Earlier, you read about ways of expressing and measuring productivity. We've established that you increase productivity by becoming more efficient. But how do you become more efficient?

Often, though not always, this involves examining work methods. Doing this might lead you to change the way the workplace is laid out, change the sequence in which things are done, change an administrative system so you can make better use of computer power and so on. The systematic examination of work methods is called **work study** – we are going to look at work study now.

The following sections will only provide a brief introduction to this rather specialized subject; they will:

- give you a taster of what work study tools and techniques are available
- provide you with some insight into the methods used by a specialist department or by outside consultants.

4.2 What is work study?

EXTENSIONS 1 AND 2
The books listed in these extensions at the end of this workbook will enable you to find out more about work study.

In most kinds of jobs efficiency depends (at least partly) on the methods used to do the work. **Work study** aims to analyse work methods and the materials and equipment used in order to:

- determine the most economical way of doing the work
- standardize the method, and install it as standard practice
- establish the time required by a qualified and trained worker to carry out the job, at a defined level of performance.

Work study has two distinct but related aspects: **method study** and **work measurement**. The following diagram gives definitions of method study and work measurement, and shows how they are used together to improve productivity and efficiency.

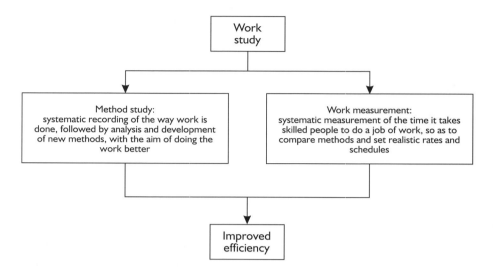

5 Method study

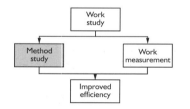

Essentially, method study involves breaking a job down into individual elements, and then analysing them. By probing and questioning, we hope to eliminate ineffective and inefficient methods and procedures and replace them with better ones.

There are six steps to method study. These are likely to overlap, but it is important that each step is completed in the sequence shown in the diagram below:

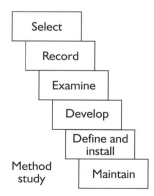

These steps can be remembered by the initial letters of the words: SREDDIM (**S**heep **r**arely **e**at **d**ead **d**aisies **i**n **M**ay).

The steps should help you:

- focus on the problem you're trying to solve
- write down your findings, so you can consider them more easily
- not to jump to conclusions
- decide what action you're going to take
- make sure your new method works, and keeps on working.

The next few pages contain a brief explanation of each of these six steps.

5.1 Select

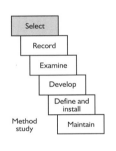

This stage is concerned with systematically examining and selecting a specific problem that needs to be solved, or an area of work that needs to be studied. The key things that must be taken into account are:

- potential savings
- investigation costs
- the extent of the resulting project – its scope and required outcomes
- the length of time that it will take to complete the project.

In selecting a problem or area the four main considerations are:

- **financial**, the impact on the organization's finances
- **technical**, where the solution is itself of a technical nature, or where the introduction of new technology forces changes in work methods to be made
- **human**, where there will be likely changes in working practices which will impact on the people concerned
- **environmental**, i.e. the impact on the local and/or wider environment.

5.2 Record

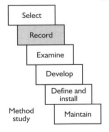

A systematic approach to method study requires systematic recording techniques. These techniques will support the person carrying out the method study in:

- recording all the relevant facts in a standardized way
- developing a clear illustration of what is happening.

Five activities have been identified which can be used to describe work activities of many kinds; each has been assigned a special symbol. The symbols are shown in the chart below.

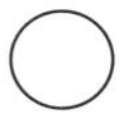 ◯	**Operation:**	(Remember 'O' for operation.)
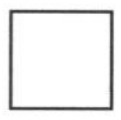 ▢	**Inspection:**	(Think of looking at something through a square window.)
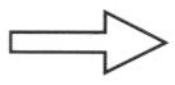 ⇨	**Transport:**	(The arrow suggests movement.)
 �◗	**Delay:**	(Looks like a 'D' for delay.)
 ▽	**Storage:**	(Imagine a cone-shaped storage container.)

There are variations on these symbols, but the ones above are the most commonly used and understood.

Consultants and work study experts use a variety of recording techniques. These include:

- **flow process diagrams** – these diagrams are drawn onto a scale diagram of the actual work area
- **string diagrams** – pins are inserted onto a scale plan of the working area. These pins will indicate nodes where, for example, work activity takes place and delays occur. Lengths of thread are used, tied between the relevant pins, to show the exact route of the work process – the total length of the thread used, in relation to the scale diagram, will be used to indicate distance materials travel, movement of people, information, etc.
- **multiple activity charts** – these are used when a team works together on any one work process. The chart will record individual team member activity in relation to a common timescale.

There are also other variations on these recording methods, and of course computer packages exist that can produce diagrammatic illustrations of these types, based on data that has been input.

5.3 Examine

The examination stage starts with a number of telling questions. By questioning, you hope to establish:

- the facts as they are
- the underlying reasons
- the alternatives
- the means by which things can be improved.

There are many questions you might ask, including:

- 'What is the purpose of the activity?'
- 'Why is it done in this location?'
- 'Why is it done by these particular people?'
- 'Why is it done in this time period?'

We can usefully categorize these questions by separating them into two sets, which we can call **primary questions** and **secondary questions**.

Primary questions concern current methods, and should relate to the following five headings:

- **purpose**: What is accomplished? Why is it necessary?
- **means**: How is it done? Why in this way?
- **place**: Where is it done? Why here?
- **sequence**: When is it done? Why at this time?
- **person**: Who does it? Why this person?

The purpose of the secondary questions is to try to propose alternative methods and to select the best of these alternatives. The options are first listed:

- What **alternative purposes** are there?
- What **alternative means** are there?
- What **alternative places** are there?
- What **alternative sequences** are there?
- What **alternative people** are there?

Then the best of these alternatives is chosen.

5.4 Development

The secondary questions trigger the development stage, which will result in a new method being selected from the proposed alternatives.

Improvement to an existing work process could be brought about by, for instance:

- eliminating a redundant activity
- modifying an activity
- combining two or more activities
- changing the location of the work
- altering the sequence of activities
- simplifying the means of doing the work.

5.5 Define and install

When the investigation has been completed, it is necessary to describe the proposed new work method in detail. This is to enable:

- the method to be installed
- training and instruction to be given
- a reference to be provided, in case of any disputes or misunderstandings, and when further changes are being considered.

Anyone investigating a problem or work area should have consulted the people involved at every stage. Installation will certainly be made more difficult if the full co-operation of those affected is not obtained.

Often it is simply not possible to switch suddenly and completely from one method of working to another.

Activity 16

You have investigated the Goods Receiving processes in place across the 23 very busy depots of your organization. It has been run as a manual system since the company was established in 1973, but your recommendation to computerise these processes has been accepted, and you have been given the go-ahead to organize purchase of the relevant hardware, software and installation of this at each of the depots.

What are three of the problems you would now have to plan to deal with?

_____

_____

_____

Your problems might include:

- how to run parallel electronic and manual systems, and for how long
- how training can happen, and how everyone concerned will receive the training without major disruption to the operation of each depot
- organizing the work area to allow the computer equipment to be installed

- issues of health and safety in terms of location of equipment.
- implementation of relevant health and safety regulatory requirements that will affect individual staff members.

Installing a new method, system or procedure may require a great deal of planning. This stage should really be considered very early on in the project, if the difficulties are to be overcome easily.

5.6 Maintain

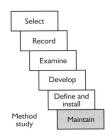

Once the new method is installed and is working properly, suitable controls should be introduced to ensure that:

- new problems are overcome as they arise
- improvements are maintained
- a regular system of feedback is established to monitor performance, targets and quality
- appropriate modifications are introduced to deal with changing conditions
- necessary paperwork actually aids the new method and does not hinder it.

Activity 17

4 mins

Perhaps you will agree that, over a period of time, agreed procedures and practices tend to be altered. From your experience of controlling work activities, what are the reasons why people tend to move away from prescribed methods? Try to list **two** reasons.

_____

_____

_____

_____

_____

_____

You may agree that people tend to alter their ways of doing things, whether consciously or unconsciously, because:

■ the agreed method does not achieve the results required. For example, a procedure that says: 'Cut the 5 metre pipe into 4 equal lengths of 1.25 metres.' might be impractical because it doesn't allow for the material lost during the cutting operation
■ the method may make the job rather awkward or tedious. Most people will tend to do work in the way that is most comfortable for them
■ circumstances change, so that the method needs to be modified.

Maintaining an installed method means making sure:

■ the method actually works in the way you think it does
■ the people involved are happy and comfortable with the method
■ the method is modified, in a controlled fashion, to deal with changing conditions
■ that management or those who commissioned or sanctioned the study are happy that the project objectives have been met.

That completes our review of method study techniques. Now we move on to the other aspect of work study: work measurement.

6 Work measurement

Imagine the following situation.

> You have started up a factory making emergency and first-aid packs. You started off in quite a small way but have become fairly successful, and are now taking on a number of new staff.
>
> You have to keep your costs to a minimum, as you have very little to play with in the pricing of your products. Some of your problems are that:
>
> ■ you want to pay your employees a bonus for meeting production targets, but don't know at what rate these bonuses should be set
> ■ you need to know what your costs are very precisely, including the time taken to carry out each task in the manufacturing process

■ you need to know how many product items can be produced each week

■ some method study investigations have been carried out, resulting in proposals for new methods of working; you now need to be able to compare these new methods with existing ones.

Managers are frequently faced with problems like these. To run a business – or any other kind of organization – successfully, it is seldom good enough to rely on broad-brush estimates: precise information is needed.

This is where work measurement can be useful.

EXTENSION 3
Operations Management
by Howard Barnett
includes a chapter on
measuring work content.

Work measurement is defined as the use of techniques to establish how long it takes a qualified worker to do a specified job to a defined level of performance.

Work measurement enables **standards** to be set so that:

■ different methods for doing a job can be compared
■ work can be organized so as to achieve optimum results using the available resources
■ incentive schemes can be reasonable and fair
■ defined cost levels can be established
■ realistic planning and estimating can be done for the future.

Work measurement is a well-established technique for providing precise information about the length of time to do a job. It is an important aid in increasing efficiency because it enables management to make accurate calculations, and enables proposed new methods to be compared.

In undertaking any form of work measurement the business will be seeking to identify and introduce methods for improving process efficiency. A range of work measurement techniques is available, with new and improved techniques being introduced all the time. Common forms include variations of:

■ time study
■ activity sampling.

6.1 Time study

This is probably the best known and most widely used technique. It involves the recording of the times and rates of working for clearly identified short elements of a job, usually by direct observation. A stopwatch or an electronic timing device is used.

The stages of time study are as follows.

1 Select the job to be studied

Ideally, **method study** should have already been applied to the job. There's no point in measuring work which is known to use inefficient procedures.

2 Break down the job into short parts or phases called **elements**

Elements are short distinct tasks (such as tightening a screw, or moving an item from one location to another). It is important that each element is separately recognizable. Normally jobs are broken down into elements which take no more than half a minute to complete.

3 Record the activity to obtain the **observed time** for each element

There are several difficulties attached to observation, not the least of which is that people tend to behave differently when they are being watched.

4 Calculate the **standard time** for the job

6.2 Activity sampling

Suppose the management of an organization want to find out the percentage of time spent on each of a number of activities. One obvious way to ascertain this information would be to set up time studies to observe the activities of each person or machine continuously over a period of time. For a large organization the cost of such an exercise would be very high indeed.

An alternative for this – and for other situations where it isn't practicable to spend large amounts of time and effort on continuous observation – is to take **sample** observations.

If, for example, a machine is being used intermittently, one approach to activity sampling would be to:

1 Observe the use of the machine over a defined period, for example one day.

2 Record the pattern of use, i.e. show when the machine is in use and when it is not on use.

3 Calculate the amount of time the machine has actually been in use. This is done by the following method:

$$\frac{\text{number of idle segments}}{\text{total number of segments}} \times 100$$

4 Carry out further observations at random points over a defined period of time, for example every fourth day in a fortnight.

This sampling approach will not give exact results, but should offer a reasonable picture of what is happening, and provide some basis for decision making.

Activity 18

5 mins

Briefly identify two advantages and two disadvantages of time study and activity sampling.

_____

_____

Advantages of time study and activity sampling are:

- an analytical approach to particular aspects of work
- a quantitative measurement, with quantitative outcomes
- if undertaken by external experts, a means of gathering objective and impartial information.

Disadvantages include:

- potentially complex types of information which is not readily understood by everyone
- statistical results of activity sampling may not be based on a relevant time period
- it separates the process from the people carrying out the process, which may result in individuals feeling alienated from resulting recommendations.

6.3 Improving process efficiency

Increasingly the emphasis has shifted from analysis of processes to the implementation of more pro-active approaches to improving overall process efficiency. Organizations have been able to compare their performance with that of their competitors, whilst encouraging staff to make suggestions on potential improvements that can be made. Continuous improvement is recognized as a more effective means of embedding change where suggestions for improvement have been made by those who are most affected by the change. This is also a far more cost-effective approach to improvement, as it can happen as and when required, in relevant and practical stages.

7 Calculating staffing requirements

Productivity is dependent to a great extent upon having the staff available to do the job required. As a team leader you will be aware of how important it is to make sure that you have enough staff available to carry out the work, and that these staff need to have the necessary skills to work effectively. A business needs to do likewise, but on a wider and longer-term basis. Human resource planning, as it is known, is concerned with forecasting what position the business will be in in the future – where its markets will be, what those markets will want – and calculating how to meet those needs in human resource terms.

The need for replacement or additional staff will arise for a number of reasons.

Activity 19   4 mins

List some of the reasons for replacing or adding new staff.

_____

_____

_____

_____

_____

_____

The reasons will include:

- changes in working practices
- staff leaving through retirement, career progression, and so on
- introduction of new technology
- increase in productivity requirements.

Productivity and quality can be negatively affected where human resource forecasting is not carried out on an ongoing basis. Think of how your area would cope if a key member of staff were to leave unexpectedly. Productivity could drop where other staff members had to step in to carry out their colleague's work, and quality could be affected too, because others may not fully understand what quality requirements are in place for that particular job role. At the same time, if staff are having to carry out more work than normal their own work levels and work quality may suffer.

You need to be constantly aware of how productivity and quality are affected by changes in staffing.

To support this human resource planning process you need to know and understand the different factors that affect your own work area. These factors are:

- numbers of staff needed to carry out current work requirements
- skills and knowledge levels required to carry out these work requirements, possibly in the form of job specifications for each role within the department or team
- potential changes to work requirements, based on information gathered
- organizational, departmental and team objectives
- number and types of staff required to fulfil these objectives.

This information is likely to be recorded in a variety of ways, with some of it being contained in staff records. You may hold this information yourself, or it may be located elsewhere. Records will need to reflect further details on team members, including:

- specific skills and knowledge of each individual in relation to work requirements
- specialist expertise – for example, first aid certificate, fork lift truck licence
- training programmes completed
- evaluation of performance – for example appraisal, performance review records
- career goals.

Activity 20

3 mins

What information do you have on your team members that can support the human resource planning process?

_____

_____

_____

_____

With this information it is possible to adapt quickly in the event of a staff member unexpectedly leaving your team. As a team leader you can consider what is required, examine the capabilities of the staff you have available, identify gaps in provision and identify where a new staff member may be required.

Using reliable and valid human resource information in the face of changes to work and work requirements will facilitate the decision-making processes and help to ensure that productivity and quality can quickly return to required levels.

Self-assessment 2

10 mins

1 The inputs to a process cost £2500, and the outputs are valued at £4500. Five people are employed on the process. Work out the overall productivity, and the output per head.

2 Insert the correct words from the list below

(a) _____ is the term used when costs are described in numerical terms or units. _____ is the term used when costs are set out in broad descriptive or less tangible terms.

(b) To justify the purchase of a new piece of equipment, or any form of change it is generally accepted that the total _____ will exceed the total costs.

(c) In undertaking any form of _____ the business will be seeking to identify and introduce methods for improving process efficiency.

(d) In the second stage of time study you will break down the job into phases called _____.

STAGES   WORK MEASUREMENT
CHARGES BENEFITS
QUALITATIVE CONSULTANCY
ELEMENTS QUANTITATIVE

3 The steps of method study have become muddled up in this diagram. Put them in the correct order.

4 What are the four main considerations, in method study, when selecting a specific problem, a problem that needs solving or an area of work that needs to be studied.

_____

_____

_____

_____

5 Identify two factors that affect managers in their own working area, in relation to human resource planning.

_____

_____

Answers to these questions can be found on page 103–4.

8 Summary

- Productivity is expressed as a ratio of what we get out for what we put in, i.e.

$$\frac{\text{output}}{\text{input}}$$

  Productivity rises if the output is increased without increasing the input, or if the output stays the same but the input is decreased.

- Cost benefit analysis methodology can be used in a range of instances, often to justify a business case.

- Work study, comprising method study and work measurement, aims to analyse work methods, and the materials and equipment used, in order to:

  - determine the most economical way of doing the work
  - standardize the method, and install it as standard practice
  - establish the time required by a qualified and trained worker to carry out the job, at a defined level of performance.

- Method study is the systematic recording of the way work is done, followed by analysis and development of the new methods, with the aim of doing the work better.

- Work measurement is the systematic measurement of the time it takes a skilled person to do a job of work, so as to compare methods and set realistic rates and schedules.

- Method study consists of the following steps:

  1 Select the problem or work area to be studied.
  2 Record what is actually taking place at the moment.
  3 Examine and analyse what has been recorded and find out any inefficiencies or shortcomings in existing methods.
  4 Develop alternatives to existing methods which are both new and improved.
  5 Define and install the new method(s).
  6 Maintain the newly installed method(s), to make sure they have achieved the required level of efficiency.

- Method study recording techniques include process charts, flow process diagrams, string diagrams and multiple activity charts.

- In undertaking any form of work measurement the business will be seeking to identify and introduce methods for improving process efficiency. A range of work measurement techniques is available, including time study and activity sampling.

- Increasingly the emphasis has shifted from analysis of processes to the implementation of more pro-active approaches to improving overall process efficiency.

- Continuous improvement is recognised as a more effective means of embedding change.

- Human resource planning is concerned with forecasting:
  - where the business will be in the future
  - where the markets will be
  - what those markets will want
  - how to meet those needs in human resource terms.

- Productivity and quality can be negatively affected where human resource forecasting is not carried out on an ongoing basis.

Session C
Efficiency in your workplace

1 Introduction

You should note that, although this session is shorter than the last, it contains a number of Activities which may involve you in several hours of work.

Terry Wisham, the Chief Executive of Clairbuoys Ltd, attended a presentation by one of his managers on the application of work study techniques to some of the organization's methods. He listened with interest, but gave a guarded response.

'OK. Supposing we spend several weeks of valuable time recording and measuring,' he said, 'working out exactly how long it should take to perform these tasks, what then? What I'm interested in is in finding efficiency improvements that are real and lasting.'

These techniques, which you read about in the last session, are useful and interesting. However, they are not magic formulae which will lead to efficiency enhancements automatically. They are practical tools which are intended to be used with careful thought and planning. If and when you do apply them, it may not be entirely apparent how they will help you in your search for increased efficiency. So what's the best approach?

You will recall that we noted in Session A that **it is in the management of resources that the key to efficiency lies**. It is therefore the aim of this next session to help you identify:

- the resources you have
- ways of planning for saving on these resources.

2 What are the real costs of using resources?

We know that maintaining and improving efficiency consists of making the best use of available resources. Now it's time for you to answer the question:

In relation to your own job and circumstances, how do you plan to 'make the best use of available resources'?

All resources have costs associated with them – the cost of purchase, the cost of use, the cost of maintenance, the cost of update or replacement, the cost of not using the resource efficiently and effectively. All organizations need to understand that a resource which is not used as it should be is a wasted resource, and as such has associated costs. In Session B we considered cost benefit analysis and so you will understand the type of costs we need to take into account.

To maximize resource efficiency a business needs to understand what resources actually cost. As a manager you need to know and understand the costs of:

- running an item of equipment
- an item of equipment lying idle
- running a faulty, poorly maintained item of equipment
- staff
- replacing staff
- producing items, and the marginal costs of producing just one more item than is required.

This is not a complete list and you can probably identify further costs that will affect the efficiency of the workplace.

First, you will need to identify the resources at your disposal.

Let's look at each type of resource in turn.

2.1 People

People are a special kind of resource. It could be said that they are the most difficult resource to develop and, if badly handled, may bring the downfall of the organization. On the other hand,

if you get your team fully motivated and working towards the right objectives, efficiency and effectiveness will follow almost automatically.

Activity 21

S/NVQs B1.1, B1.2

This Activity, together with a later one (Activity 27 on page 59), will provide you with a basis for a structured approach to increasing efficiency, by finding ways to advance the potential of your team.

This Activity may provide the basis of appropriate evidence for your S/NVQ portfolio. Whether or not you decide to do this, you may like to use these two Activities as a basis for a plan of your own; you can come back to them periodically when you are thinking about possible improvements in efficiency.

Use a separate sheet of paper for this Activity.

Write down the names and brief details of your team members. If you feel you know an individual reasonably well, just jot down in brief notes his or her main skills and experience. (Remember, this is for your own benefit, and no one else's.) If you find this difficult, it may be that you need to find out more about the person concerned; in this case, remind yourself of the fact.

Then try to think of at least one kind of task that you think each person is capable of performing, that he or she does not currently do.

Set out your sheet of paper as follows, repeated for as many people as you have in your team.

Name and main job function	Brief summary of skills and experience
	I need to get to know more about this team member ☐
This person has the potential to:	

2.2 Workspace

We listed land and buildings among the main resources of organizations, but when it gets down to individual teams it is more appropriate to talk about workspace.

Activity 22 · 10+ mins

S/NVQs B1.1, B1.2

This Activity, together with a later one (Activity 28 on page 60), is designed to help you to make optimum use of your workspace.

This Activity may provide the basis of appropriate evidence for your S/NVQ portfolio.

Your next task is to study the workspace which you are able to use.

It may be appropriate to draw a plan, if your team all work in one area. Alternatively, you could just make a list. Remember that your eventual aim is to find better ways of using your workspace.

(For some managers, for example those who lead teams who are travelling most of the time, or who spend their time on other organizations' premises, this Activity may not be very meaningful. If this is the case with you, ignore it.)

2.3 Machinery and equipment

When we consider machinery and equipment we generally have to take into account a variety of items, ranging from simple tools to complex machinery. Simple tools tend to be reliable, and at the same time they do not require costly maintenance, however, they do still have to be available to support the work that needs to be done. Machinery and more complex equipment may form the essential foundation of a key work process, for example computerised telephone systems in call centres – without these the purpose of the business cannot be fulfilled.

The purpose of the next Activity is to identify essential equipment and machinery in your work area, then to consider the use of each item, as well as any problems encountered.

Activity 23

S/NVQs B1.1, B1.2

This Activity, together with a later one (Activity 29 on page 61) will provide you with a basis for a structured approach to increased efficiency in the use of machinery and equipment.

This Activity may provide the basis of appropriate evidence for your S/NVQ portfolio.

Use a separate sheet of paper for this Activity.

Compile a list of all the essential equipment and machinery within your area of work. The items that you identify must be essential to the overall fulfillment of the purpose of your work area, that is, without the item the work could not continue and objectives could not be achieved.

For each item ask the following questions:

- What is it used for?
- Who uses it?
- How frequently is the item used?
- How easy is it to use (how much training and support)?
- What problems have we had with this item over the past week, month, quarter?
- How quickly was the problem resolved?
- What maintenance (in terms of frequency and complexity) is required?

To make this Activity more effective you might want to involve your team members in compiling the list and in answering the questions.

2.4 Materials and components

Now we come to the things that get used up in the transformation process.

Activity 24 · 15+ mins

S/NVQs B1.1, B1.2

This Activity, together with a later one (Activity 30 on page 62), will provide you with a basis for a structured approach to increased efficiency in the use of materials.

This Activity may provide the basis of appropriate evidence for your S/NVQ portfolio.

Identify the materials and components that are the inputs to your team's work process, together with any consumables.

This time, it might be relevant to also note down your current wastage rate for each item, if you know it. (There may be a number of reasons why wastage occurs, apart from spoiled material. For example, a team servicing computers will need to carry parts, some of which may become outdated before they are used.) Wastage is covered in detail in Session D.

Again, make the list as detailed as you feel is appropriate for your needs. If you are able to write down this list without reference to other sources, a quick summary may be all that's required. But if you are not clear about what kinds of materials are used by your workteam, it could be a good idea to do some research on the subject.

Use a separate sheet of paper as before.

2.5 Energy

The amount of energy your team uses can be measured by your fuel utilization. The difficulty with identifying this resource is that, typically, electricity and other forms of fuel will be shared with others in the organization. It is more productive to discuss ways of saving energy, and we'll leave discussion of this resource until later in the session.

2.6 Time

Time is allocated to everyone equally, and yet is still very precious. Perhaps it is not a good idea to ask you to identify how much time you have to spare, as you may decide to leave the paper blank!

2.7 Finance

The amount of financial responsibility given to team leaders and first-line managers varies considerably. For the next Activity, you are asked to write down the extent of your own authority to handle finances.

Activity 25   5 mins

How much scope do you have when it comes to spending the organization's money?

(a) How large a budget do you control, if any, and what kind of items are you permitted to buy or hire?

_____

_____

_____

(b) If you do not have your own budget, how much practical, effective control do you have over the purchase of materials, the hiring of people, etc.? (For example, you may not officially be a signatory on documents that authorize the spending of money, but your recommendations may, to some extent, be accepted without question.)

_____

_____

_____

(c) To what degree do you feel your efforts are being frustrated by the lack of control you have over finances? Do you think you could make your team more efficient if you were able to make more financial decisions, for example? If so, how could you persuade your manager of this?

_____

_____

_____

2.8 Information

This is the last item on our list of resources. Sources and types of information are many and varied, and are therefore difficult to summarize. Instead, you are asked to identify deficiencies.

Activity 26 · 15+ mins

S/NVQs B1.1, B1.2

This Activity, together with a later one (Activity 32 on pages 64–5), will provide you with a basis for a structured approach to increasing efficiency by improving your sources of information.

This Activity may provide the basis of appropriate evidence for your S/NVQ portfolio. If you are intending to take this course of action, it might be better to write your answers on separate sheets of paper.

What kinds of additional information, if any, would help you and your team do your job more efficiently? Answer the following questions by encircling your response and explaining it briefly.

(a) Would you or your team work more efficiently if you were given more information about the processes or procedures you work with?   Yes/No

Explain: _____

_____

_____

(b) Would you or your team work more efficiently if you were given more information about the activities of other teams or other parts of the organization?   Yes/No

Explain: _____

_____

_____

(c) Is there any other kind of information that would help to make you or your team work more efficiently?   Yes/No

Explain: _____

_____

_____

3 Planning for improved efficiency and effectiveness

Now that you have spent some time analysing and identifying the resources that are currently available to you, it is time to start making plans to:

- utilize those resources in a better way
- obtain additional resources that would help to make you or your team more efficient
- increase your effectiveness.

This section looks at how to maximise the use of available resources. This will involve planning and evaluation, and building, on the information which you produced in completing the Activities in section 2.

Plans will need to take into account the costs associated with the required actions, but at the same time demonstrable benefits should result from taking the planned actions.

3.1 People

There are many approaches to the management task of getting the best from people. Here are a few ideas to add to your own.

■ Training

Often, individuals feel frustrated at not being able to carry out their work as efficiently and effectively as they would like, because they have not been fully trained. Training may consist of specific instructions and guidance regarding a particular process or procedure, such as how to operate a machine, how to use some computer software, or the safest method of evacuating a building. These are the technical skills.

Your team may also require training in financial, administrative or inter-personal skills.

But remember, too, that the training needs of your team may have more to do with their lack of understanding of the principles, or the rationale behind the work they are asked to do, than the development of specific skills. Thinking people want to know more than **how** to do something, they need to know **why**. For example:

- cooks and chefs need to understand the concepts behind nutrition, as well as cooking methods and recipes
- accountants in a manufacturing company will do a better job if they have a good appreciation of the processes they are being asked to cost
- health club instructors may improve their performance if they are trained to explain the effects of particular exercises on the body, rather than simply showing visitors how to use gym equipment.

Training sessions do not need to be expensive, although it is important that they are conducted in a professional manner.

■ Coaching

A coach is someone who aims to get the best out of people: the best efforts, the best achievements, the best ideas.

By coaching you can:

- convey the objectives of the organization and the team, so that everyone works to the same ends and in the same direction
- create an atmosphere in which the team is encouraged to work out its own solutions to problems, through understanding, not by simply following a rigid set of steps
- get people to believe in themselves, and their ability to improve their efficiency and effectiveness.

■ Empowering and delegating

The modern concept of a manager is primarily as leader – someone who sets out to gain trust, influence and commitment, and is prepared to give respect and power to the team.

It is the team who must get the job done, and it is the leader's role to provide them with the means to do it: to empower them.

Virtually any and every task can be delegated.

Activity 27   15+ mins

S/NVQs B1.1, B1.2

This Activity, together with Activity 21 on page 51, will provide you with a basis for a structured approach to increasing efficiency, by finding ways to advance the potential of your team.

This Activity may provide the basis of appropriate evidence for your S/NVQ portfolio.

In Activity 21, you were asked to make notes about the members of your team. Now you should use your response to decide what actions to take in order to get the best from these resources. Use the following questions to help you make your decisions. Write your answers on separate sheets of paper.

(a) What training will you arrange for each of your team members, that will help them to become more efficient or effective? Skills training (technical, administrative, financial, interpersonal)? Education, to give greater awareness and understanding?

(b) How will you start coaching people to achieve their objectives, and to believe in themselves and their ability to solve their own problems?

(c) How do you intend to delegate more tasks, and to empower the team to achieve more?

3.2 Workspace

Badly used workspace can result in:

■ **congestion** – if workstations are too close together, for example

■ **accidents** – if there is not enough room, corridors aren't clearly marked, or gangways are blocked

■ **inefficient communications** – when people can't see each other, when there is too much noise, or when too many people have to use the same phone

■ **excessive energy costs** – when doors and windows are left open, or a building is badly insulated

■ **low production** – if there are breaks and discontinuities in the flow.

Activity 28 · 15+ mins

S/NVQs B1.1, B1.2

This Activity, together with Activity 22 on page 52, is designed to help you to make optimum use of your workspace.

This Activity may provide the basis of appropriate evidence for your S/NVQ portfolio.

In Activity 22, you set out the workspace available to your team. In doing so, you may have thought up some ideas of the ways in which you might improve the use of the available space, or some means of acquiring additional space.

Now set up a meeting with your team about this subject. What problems do they see? How would they solve them? (You may be able to delegate this whole task, and take on the role of coach and facilitator.)

Write down the results of your meeting on a separate sheet of paper, and say what your next step will be.

3.3 Machinery and equipment

Earlier (in Activity 23), you were asked to list the essential equipment and machinery your team uses, and to identify any problems with it. Now's the time to think about ways of solving those problems, and of utilizing these items more efficiently.

Activity 29 · 30+ mins

S/NVQs B1.1, B1.2

This Activity will provide you with a basis for a structured approach to making better use of your work equipment.

This Activity may provide the basis of appropriate evidence for your S/NVQ portfolio.

Consultation with your team will help to establish practical and supported approaches to using machinery and equipment more effectively and efficiently.

Review the information gathered in Activity 23, focusing in particular on the following questions.

■ How long is the item left idle – and why?
■ What maintenance-related problems have we experienced?
■ What other common problems have arisen regularly?

Reflect on the results from this analysis. Where possible calculate the costs, qualitative and quantitative, of:

■ idle equipment
■ maintenance-related problems
■ other common problems.

Now build a plan for tackling each of these areas. This plan should show what action is needed, and the estimated costs of such action. You may also wish to produce a formal maintenance schedule where it is clear that maintenance is a core problem with wide-ranging costs. A maintenance schedule can be established which takes account of peak working times, shift patterns and manufacturers' guidance (remember: warranties may only apply where proof of regular maintenance is available). As you have already learned, maintenance will have costs, but the benefits are likely to far outweigh these.

3.4 Materials and components

As already mentioned, there may be a good deal of scope for making savings on materials and components.

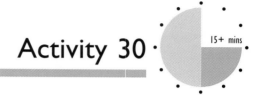

Activity 30

S/NVQs B1.1, B1.2

This Activity, together with Activity 24 on page 54, will provide you with a basis for a structured approach to increased efficiency in the use of materials.

This Activity may provide the basis of appropriate evidence for your S/NVQ portfolio.

Following your response to Activity 24, you need now to help the work team find ways of optimizing the use of the materials and components you use. Prompt responses from your work team members by posing the following questions:

(a) How can we reduce wastage of materials and consumables?

(b) Are the materials and components we use the best ones for the job?

(c) If the answer to (b) is no, how can we identify and obtain better ones?

(d) Are the processes we use making the best use of the materials and components?

(e) If the answer to (d) is no, how can the processes be improved?

(f) Are our end products what our customers want?

(g) If the answer to (f) is no, what can we do about it?

3.5 Energy

The key to efficiency when it comes to energy use is simple: save as much of it as possible.

Activity 31

10+ mins

S/NVQs B1.1, B1.2

Use the following checklist to help you find ways of saving energy. (The 'you' in this Activity refers to you personally, or any member of your team.) Tick the boxes.

	Yes	No
(a) Do you know how much energy you are using?	☐	☐
(b) If not, can you find out and bring it to the attention of the team, so you can monitor improvements?	☐	☐
(c) Do you take trouble to ensure that heating, lights and machinery are switched off when they aren't needed?	☐	☐
(d) Is there a proper system of maintenance for boilers and other energy-consuming equipment?	☐	☐
(e) Do you keep doors and windows closed during the winter months?	☐	☐
(f) Does the building where you work have efficient heat insulation?	☐	☐
(g) Do you encourage or reward the saving of energy?	☐	☐

Now give your own ideas for saving energy:

_____

_____

_____

_____

_____

Finally, on separate sheets, write down the steps you are going to take to make savings in energy.

3.6 Finances

An overall measure of efficiency, and the one that accountants and chief executives are inclined to use, is the amount of profit made by the organization this year as compared to last. In simple terms, the input is the amount of money put into the enterprise, and the output is the amount of income. The difference is the profit.

The best way to save money is to become more efficient in the use of your resources.

If you are responsible for a budget, you may need to improve your administration and control procedures. You could perhaps:

■ keep better records of expenditure and the use of materials, ensuring they are complete, accurate and accessible
■ ensure you monitor and maintain resources such as equipment and materials in accordance with organizational requirements
■ keep your team members informed of their individual responsibilities for the control of resources
■ ensure that, if you need to make spending decisions which thereby exceed your budget, you refer to your line manager or other relevant authority.

3.7 Information

The next (and last) Activity on the efficient use of resources requires you to plan to find the information you and your team need.

Activity 32

S/NVQs B1.1, B1.2

This Activity, together with Activity 26 on page 56, will provide you with a basis for a structured approach to increasing efficiency by improving your sources of information.

This Activity may provide the basis of appropriate evidence for your S/NVQ portfolio.

In Activity 26 you made notes on the kind of information you think you are lacking in. Now explain how you intend to obtain this additional or alternative information.

_____

_____

_____

Self-assessment 3

10 mins

I   Fill in the blanks in the following sentences with suitable words chosen from the list below.

(a)   If you get your team fully _____ and working towards the right _____, efficiency and effectiveness will follow almost automatically.

(b)   A _____ is someone who aims to get the best out of people: the best _____, the best _____, the best _____.

(c)   It is the _____ who must get the job done, and it is the _____'s role to provide them with the means to do it: to _____ them.

(d)   Badly used workspace can result in _____, _____, inefficient _____, excessive _____ costs or low _____.

ACCIDENTS	EFFORTS	MOTIVATED
ACHIEVEMENTS	EMPOWER	OBJECTIVES
COACH	ENERGY	PRODUCTION
COMMUNICATIONS	IDEAS	TEAM
CONGESTION	LEADER	

2 List **four** ways to save energy for someone who works in an office.

_____

_____

_____

_____

3 Make **three** suggestions for controlling finances better, for someone who controls a budget for a small department.

_____

_____

_____

_____

4 Give **three** examples of costs associated with the use of resources.

_____

_____

_____

_____

Answers to these questions can be found on page 104.

4 Summary

This session has mainly consisted of suggestions and Activities designed to help you and your work team become more efficient and effective. Among the questions posed were the following.

- Do you know and understand the costs of:
  - running an item of equipment
  - an item of equipment lying idle
  - running a faulty, poorly maintained item of equipment
  - staff
  - replacing staff
  - producing items, and producing just one more item than required?

- Is your use of people efficient and effective? Are they:
  - trained to perform their assigned tasks
  - enabled to develop their skills
  - empowered to take control of their work?

- Could you delegate more tasks?

- Are you, the manager, acting as a leader who not only sets out to gain trust, influence and commitment, but is also prepared to give respect and power to the team?

- How can you utilize your workspace in a more efficient and effective way, so as to avoid:
  - congestion
  - accidents
  - inefficient communications
  - excessive energy costs
  - low levels of production?

- How can you improve your management of equipment and machinery? Is there some that:
  - is under-utilized
  - is in a poor state of repair
  - is badly suited for the task it is used for
  - you understand the operation of insufficiently?

- If you are responsible for a budget, how can you improve your administration and control procedures? Could you perhaps:
  - keep better records of expenditure and the use of materials, ensuring they are complete, accurate and accessible
  - ensure you monitor and maintain resources such as equipment and materials in accordance with organizational requirements
  - keep your team members informed of their individual responsibilities for the control of resources
  - ensure that, if you need to make spending decisions which thereby exceed your budget, you refer to your line manager or other relevant authority?

- Would you or your work team work more efficiently if you were given more information about the processes or procedures you work with?

- Would you or your work team work more efficiently if you were given more information about the activities of other teams or other parts of the organization?

- Is there any other kind of information that would help to make you or your work team work more efficiently?

Session D
Managing waste

1 Introduction

Within every type of organization the processes of work will result in waste.

Valuable resources can be wasted in a number of ways, including:

- misuse – used for a purpose for which they were not designed, resulting in inefficiency and shortages for their intended purpose
- extravagance – where a resource is being consumed even though it is not necessary in order to achieve objectives
- scrap – items left over as a result of a production process which cannot be readily used elsewhere
- rework – where items have to be remade because they failed quality controls.
- shrinkage – where the resource is consumed in unauthorized ways (often used as a euphemism for 'theft'), where it deteriorates in quality over time, or simply becomes obsolescent.

Elimination of waste will not be practical across all work processes, but reduction of waste in many of these is desirable.

Types of waste will fall within the four categories of resource examined throughout this workbook. These categories are:

- people
- capital
- materials
- information.

We usually associate the idea of waste with the materials resource category. Although we will focus on this particular aspect of waste for the purpose of this session it is important not to lose sight of the fact that waste can, and does, occur in each of the remaining three categories.

EXTENSION 4
A useful website giving information about waste management is given at the end of this workbook.

People are not used efficiently across the work processes, whether we consider manufacturing or service industries. Individual capabilities are not always recognized and used to best effect, or development is not offered to enable individuals to maximize their contribution to the business as a whole; and so there is waste. Business assets or capital may be misused because they are not always suitable or appropriate to the current or future needs of that business. The business may not invest sufficiently in its equipment or machinery, requiring staff to spend time repairing or 'making-do', resulting in customer dissatisfaction and ultimately loss of money, another example of waste.

Information produces waste as well, in situations where businesses do not gather, exchange or indeed use information in a way which is relevant to how the business functions. Many businesses suffer from information overload, where there is a great deal of information available, but not enough that exists in the detail and format that everyone can use efficiently. This is a clear, and common example of waste.

This session will focus primarily on the area of materials waste, exploring methods for measuring and monitoring it, as well as setting out practical approaches to the minimizing of it.

2 Waste control legislation

A range of regulations and legislation are in place in relation to waste disposal which will have varying levels of impact on your own area of work.

The European Union has passed legislation to underpin and improve waste handling controls, including:

- Packaging Waste Regulations
- Landfill Levy
- Fridges and Ozone Depleting Regulations
- Environmental Protection Act (1990).

Activity 33 · 10 mins

Which of these legislative and regulatory areas apply to your organization as a whole, and to your area of work in particular?

_____

_____

_____

Briefly describe what the requirements are. (You may need to talk to your manager or human resources department to get this information.)

_____

_____

_____

_____

How do you currently ensure that your area of work conforms to the regulations as required?

_____

_____

How satisfied are you that you and your staff understand the implications of these regulations and laws?

_____

_____

Although the nature of your business may not necessitate you understanding the requirements of each of these items, within each there may be aspects which apply, and which will affect your plans for waste reduction and waste disposal.

3 The costs of waste

There are a range of costs associated with waste, its production and its minimization.

Waste has costs that are usually stated in terms of monetary loss to the organization. Most organizations rarely calculate the true monetary cost of waste. The Environment Agency considers that the actual cost of waste can be as high as 5 – 10 per cent of company turnover (Source: The Environment Agency; *www.environment-agency.gov.uk* June 2002). Businesses regularly underestimate the cost of waste to their business and in doing so have no clear picture as to real loss of profit.

Activity 34

4 mins

Other than the monetary cost of waste what other costs can you identify? Try to make three suggestions.

_____

_____

_____

You could have mentioned:

- rework of poorly finished items
- lost stock – raw material, contributory items
- quality and reduced customer satisfaction
- waste handling and disposal
- environmental – within the company and on a wider basis
- need for protective clothing, monitoring and handling equipment, where hazardous substances form part of the work process
- insurance to cover liabilities in relation to waste disposal and emissions
- monitoring of waste.

You may have identified others which are relevant to your area of work, and which do not appear in the above list.

The Environment Agency offers a definition of the true cost of materials waste as:

'the cost of the raw material in the waste added to the cost of disposal'.

In a wider sense we could include labour, processes, energy, consumables, etc. within the 'raw materials' description to get a clearer indication of what needs to be considered.

In a production scenario we would need to calculate this cost in relation to every item produced, which can seem both time consuming and potentially difficult. If businesses fail to carry out this calculation they lose sight of where savings can be made and where money can be reclaimed within the work processes. In terms of a service situation the calculation is as valid, if not as apparently straightforward.

Activity 35 · 3 mins

All contributory factors within a work process need to be taken into account when calculating the cost of waste.

Within a service sector business, what might be included in the term 'raw materials' when examining the definition of materials waste?

_____

_____

_____

The list is extensive, but could include factors such as:

- time, possibly including travel time where, for example, sales people need to visit client premises
- people, where staff regularly find themselves with insufficient work to do
- information, including too much irrelevant information
- access to equipment, such as computers and telephones
- consumables, such as stationery
- fuel for vehicles, again relating to the example of salespeople travelling.

4 A staged approach to managing waste

The most important part of implementing any programme of waste reduction is to gain the commitment of both senior management **and** all staff.

Commitment from senior management will support any need for using time, and possibly the need for capital investment, where this proves essential. Staff commitment will reduce any potential barriers that may lie in the way of programme success.

Waste reduction is an ongoing process and is less likely to succeed where it is perceived as a one-off initiative. Contributions from everyone will form the basis of this success. As we have already identified the costs of waste and the factors affecting waste permeate all aspects of work, and so everyone can make active contributions to waste reduction.

The stages in managing waste are as follows:

1   Awareness raising

2   Process analysis

3   Clarifying costs

4   Future planning

5   Defining the problem and identifying solutions

6   Taking action.

These stages do not stand alone. For example, awareness raising cannot be a stage in its own right, as it is essential that everyone is made constantly aware of the issues, while being informed as to the actions they will need to take.

We will explore each of these stages in some detail so that you can consider how you might proceed with each one in your own area of work.

5 Awareness raising

An awareness campaign that sets out the benefits of waste reduction, while emphasizing the range of costs associated with waste, is a useful way of focusing attention on waste minimization. Individuals can be encouraged to identify sources of waste in their own area, and to offer suggestions for how waste might be reduced. It is important to encourage enthusiasm for the whole idea of waste reduction, but it can be all too easy for this to become a one-off campaign which quickly loses momentum and which is not deemed an important everyday issue.

A waste reduction awareness campaign can usefully kick-start awareness raising. Ongoing reminders of the importance of waste reduction will be essential to keeping the process alive within the business.

Activity 36 · · 3 mins

List three advantages of reducing waste that you believe would arouse staff interest in supporting a waste reduction programme.

_____

_____

_____

The advantages will vary greatly from business to business, team to team. Some of the ideas you had might have included:

- reduced frustration when less time has to be spent having to rework badly finished products
- reduction in customer complaints because the quality of service and products improves

■ heightened respect from the community where they see the business investing in improving the local environment through improved approaches to waste disposal.

Each of these points arises from the success of different waste reduction programmes in different types of organization. Using these ideas you may now wish to go back to the activity you have just finished and add further ideas for arousing staff interest.

6 Process analysis

In order to analyse each of the work processes in your area you will need to consider the following questions.

■ What kinds of waste are produced from this area of work?
■ How much of each type of waste is produced on a weekly/monthly/quarterly/ annual basis?
■ What methods of waste disposal are used?
■ What environmental requirements do we need to take into account when disposing of business waste?

Activity 37 · 10+ mins

S/NVQs B1.1, B1.2

This Activity may provide the basis of appropriate evidence for your S/NVQ portfolio. Write your answers on separate sheets of paper.

Design a form that covers each of the above questions and has sufficient space for responses. (For the second question you might want to limit the time scales, for example you may just ask for information regarding waste production on a monthly basis). Then issue the form to key individuals within each area of work which falls within your supervision, and ask them to complete it and return it to you.

One obvious means of raising awareness is to involve staff in gathering responses to these questions. Again, the nature of the business will affect certain responses to a greater degree than it will do in others. However, this type of investigation will not only heighten awareness, but will help to inform where the business has fallen into bad habits, or indeed where the business has failed to take account of the ever-increasing environmental legislation which affects it.

The responses to the questions will help in identifying the range of actual work processes which produce waste. Process analysis is a method of mapping out each of the actions that go into any work process. For example, reflect on the inputs, transformations and outputs diagram on page 3 and your response to Activity 2. Each of the examples can be broken down into yet more detailed processes.

We will use the following illustration as an example of how a process can be analysed.

A chiropodist will need an appointment system in order to improve people by attending to their feet. The stages in this chiropodist-client booking process may include:

Stage 1   advertise chiropody service in local paper/mailshot to existing clients.

Stage 2   receive phone calls from clients.

Stage 3   input appointments into diary (book or computer).

Stage 4   greet clients and place them in waiting room.

Stage 5   take clients through to chiropodist.

A flowchart is an effective and efficient means of carrying out and illustrating process analysis.

One way of illustrating each stage of this process is by producing a flowchart. Each box of the flowchart will contain a separate stage, with arrows going between each in the relevant direction.

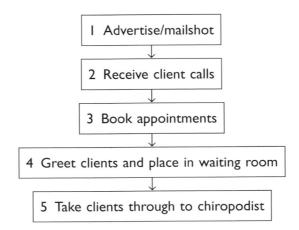

1 Advertise/mailshot

2 Receive client calls

3 Book appointments

4 Greet clients and place in waiting room

5 Take clients through to chiropodist

To develop a fuller analysis of each process you can include detail on which raw materials are needed at each stage. For example, in stage 2 above (receive phone calls from clients) such materials would include a telephone, receptionist and, probably a computer.

Example:

> 2 Receive phone calls from clients
> *receptionist*
> *telephone*
> *notepad/computer/diary*

In order for the process analysis to be thorough the flowchart will need to show:

- each stage in the process
- the raw materials and resources needed for each step.

As well as this information the flowchart will also need to show points where waste is or could be produced.

These points can appear as crosses or exclamation marks next to the box containing the relevant stage.

Example: Chiropodist client booking process

> 3 Greet clients and place in waiting room
> *receptionist*
> *chairs*
> *magazines/radio/sound system!*

From the information gathered earlier, possibly by using questionnaires as designed in Activity 37, you will have a clear indication of where waste occurs and the nature of this waste.

Activity 38 ·

Why do you believe an exclamation mark might appear next to stage 3 in the chiropodist–client booking process?

_____

_____

You may have said that, assuming that there is only one chiropodist available, there is never likely to be more than one client waiting at any one time. The size of the waiting room may be over and above that required, and the space may be better used by increasing the reception area itself, or even by giving the space to the chiropodist through reorganization of the existing space. At the same time if there is only one client the sound system may be superfluous, when up-to-date magazines would allow the client to fill in the short waiting time quite adequately.

The number of stages in each process will vary, and so of course will the complexity of the resulting flowchart. It is important to try and keep the process analysis simple and easy to understand – your flowcharts will provide valuable visual information to others, and serve to illustrate points of actual or potential waste.

Activity 39 ·

S/NVQ B1.2

Refer back to the completed forms that asked individuals to identify types and sources of waste (Activity 37). From this information identify up to three separate work processes. Choose one of these and draw a flowchart that clearly illustrates:

- ■ each stage in the process
- ■ raw materials and resources required at each stage
- ■ points where waste is or could be produced.

7 Clarifying costs

This stage in the waste minimization process refers you back to the information in section 3, *The costs of waste*, and to the work that you have already done in Activity 37. You were asked to consider the real costs of waste within your area of work. Now reconsider these in the light of the detail offered in section 6, *Process analysis*.

Activity 40

20+ mins

S/NVQ B1.2

This Activity may provide the basis of appropriate evidence for your S/NVQ portfolio. Whether or not you are intending to take this course of action, it might be better to write your answers on separate sheets of paper.

Refer back to the flowchart which you produced for Activity 39.

1 List the types of cost associated with this process. If possible provide detail of the actual costs (for example, costs of receptionist) on an hourly basis.

2 Now consider the location of waste production and estimate the potential cost of this waste where it is identified. For example, provision of a superfluous sound system.

3 Where waste disposal is associated with waste, estimate the costs of waste disposal across the complete process.

You may or may not have detailed information to support the completion of this activity, but even if you are only able to estimate the costs you will be building a clearer picture of the real costs of waste.

Activity 41 · 5 mins

S/NVQ B1.1

Reconsider your flowchart. What potential or actual cost savings might be the result of any waste reduction, where it has been identified as feasible?

Type of potential waste reduction	Potential/actual costs savings

As others become more actively involved in identifying and tackling issues of waste, waste-related costs will reduce accordingly.

8 Future planning

If you have already identified a number of areas for immediate waste reduction, or are in the process of taking the necessary action to reduce waste effectively and efficiently, it is likely that you are already seeing signs of increased efficiency across the work processes that you have analysed. In order to develop efficiency overall there will be some areas where immediate action is not practical. Any list that you have started to build will need to be prioritised, so that a resulting action plan, as at stage 6 of the waste management process, will take account of the necessary resources.

When establishing priorities for your list, consider the following questions.

■ What are the immediate costs of reducing waste?
■ What capital costs might be needed?
■ What disposal costs are attached to waste reduction?

■ What environmental impact will result from the waste reduction, for example are there any proposed process changes or materials usage that will fall within legal or regulatory controls?

■ What impact will these changes have on other work processes, and will this hinder efficiency elsewhere?

(Based on The Environment Agency 9 Step Process for Waste Minimization, June 2002.)

By involving other members of your team in considering these questions, you will not only develop support for these proposed changes, you will also access their knowledge of the particular issues.

It is important to remember that this list of potential waste reduction areas is in fact a list of potential changes. The earlier you can involve others in determining feasibility the more likely any changes are to succeed.

9 Defining the problem and identifying solutions

This is another stage that does not fit neatly into a strict process. This stage involves identifying **why** waste is the result of particular stages in the work process, and then identifying how best to reduce this waste. As you will realize this will already have begun to happen throughout the other stages, particularly during process analysis.

Activity 42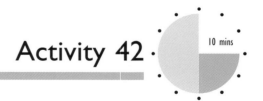

Identify two areas where waste is being generated (you might want to refer to the flowchart which you drew in response to Activity 39), and briefly respond to the following questions for each area.

■ What is happening to create this waste?

■ When is the waste being generated; at exactly which stage of the work process?

■ What would happen further down the work process if this level of waste were eliminated?

Area 1 _____

_____

_____

Area 2 _____

_____

_____

9.1 Cause and effect

We are now coming to the point of considering the causes of the waste and its effect.

Activity 43 · 25 mins

S/NVQ B1.2

This Activity may provide the basis of appropriate evidence for your S/NVQ portfolio. If you are intending to take this course of action, it might be better to write your answers on separate sheets of paper.

Discuss your responses to the previous activity with others within your team. Now ask them the following questions.

It is important to prioritise any list of potential changes; involving others in this process will ensure that resulting changes are dealt with positively.

■ What is the actual cause of the waste that is being generated?
■ What is the real effect of the waste?

Write a full description of the actual cause and the real effect of the waste that is being generated. Your aim is to write a description that gives a thorough picture of the situation. This description becomes your definition of the waste reduction issue. Try and write the definition in language which makes sense to everyone concerned, in this way you will help people relate to what is required, helping them to feel that they can make a sound contribution to any proposed solutions.

A good and clear definition of the waste reduction issue will provide a useful starting point for arriving at practical solutions.

Once the waste reduction issue has been clearly defined it is essential to identify reasonable and practical solutions to this issue. As stated earlier it will be beneficial to involve others, drawing on their knowledge and expertise of the issue, its causes and its effects.

Activity 44 · 1 hour

Call a meeting of those who are affected by the waste reduction issue, or perhaps involved in the cause. Ask: what can we do to address this waste reduction issue? Produce a list of **all** the suggestions offered.

Consult everyone, exploring the suggestions on the list.

Through this consultation:

1   Eliminate those suggestions which are obviously impractical or ill-advised.

2   Rank the remaining suggestions in three groups where group 1 = most practical, group 2 = practical and group 3 = feasible.

The resulting list will be a ranked list of suggestions which already have the support both of those concerned and of those who are essential to the success of any changes made.

10 Taking action

By this stage you will have comprehensive information on the points where waste is being generated, a definition of the causes and effects of this waste generation, and a list of potential solutions or means of waste reduction. You will have realized that stages 4, 5 and 6 are closely inter-linked.

You are now in a position to create an action plan to reduce the identified waste. We have given an example of an action plan below.

Waste reduction Issue	Action required	Responsible person	Time scale	Review date	Evaluation	Desired outcome
1. Reduce quantity of A4 copier paper rejected at office copier and thrown into wastepaper bins	a. Set up copy logging system	Andi	w/c 12 June	17 June	Log completed and register numbers tally	Reduce copier paper orders by 5% within next two quarters
	b. Collect re-usable paper from copier and staple into notepads	Ben	Twice daily from w/c 12 June	Twice weekly from w/c 12 June	Only paper which cannot be salvaged to be found in wastepaper bins	
	c. Train all office staff in use of photocopiers to reduce errors	Ellie	Completed by 26 June	26 June	All staff able to operate photocopier and reduce errors of use	

As a means of ensuring that action is taken regularly and on an ongoing basis, a simple action plan will establish:

- the waste reduction issue
- steps required to reduce the waste
- who has responsibility for taking the necessary steps
- timescales against which the steps will be taken
- milestone points, review dates
- methods of evaluation
- desired outcome.

Activity 45

5 mins

What can you do to ensure that your waste reduction action plans are implemented? Try to make three suggestions.

_____

_____

_____

Waste reduction can only result from practical and well-considered action.

You will have recognized that the key factors in ensuring action plan implementation will include:

- sound definition of the waste reduction issue, which everyone concerned can understand and relate to
- a series of realistic stages that will result in waste reduction
- allocation of responsibility for different stages given to those who are able to take the necessary action
- ensuring that those with allocated responsibility have the relevant authority and access to the necessary resources
- review dates adhered to
- evaluation methods suited to the types of action required
- the desired outcome set in terms that are measurable.

Self-assessment 4 · 10 mins

Fill in the blanks in the following sentences with suitable words chosen from the list below.

(a) Most organizations rarely calculate the true _____ cost of waste.

(b) All _____ factors within a work process need to be taken into account when calculating the cost of waste.

(c) A waste reduction _____ can usefully kick-start awareness raising. Ongoing reminders of the _____ of waste reduction will be essential to keeping the process alive within the business.

(d) A _____ definition of the waste reduction issue will provide a useful starting point for arriving at practical _____.

RELEVANT	GOOD AND CLEAR	FINANCIAL
CONTRIBUTORY	SMART	MONETARY
ENJOYMENT	AWARENESS CAMPAIGN	SOLUTIONS
IMPORTANCE	RESULTS	

2   List the six stages in managing waste reduction.

_____

_____

_____

_____

_____

_____

3   Identify three key factors in ensuring that waste reduction action plans are implemented.

_____

_____

_____

Answers to these questions can be found on page 105

11 Summary

- The costs which result from the generation of waste include:
  - monetary cost of waste
  - rework of poorly finished items
  - lost stock – raw material, contributory items
  - quality and reduced customer satisfaction
  - waste handling and disposal
  - environmental – within the company and on a wider basis
  - need for protective clothing, monitoring and handling equipment
  - insurance to cover liabilities in relation to waste disposal and emissions
  - monitoring of waste.

- Waste reduction is an ongoing process, rather than just a one-off initiative.

- By adopting a staged approach to waste reduction, success is more likely.

- A staged model for waste reduction includes the following six stages:
  1. awareness raising
  2. process analysis
  3. clarifying costs
  4. future planning
  5. defining the problem and identifying solutions
  6. taking action.

- An awareness campaign that sets out the benefits of waste reduction while emphasizing the range of costs associated with waste is a useful way of focusing attention on waste minimization.

- Process analysis includes questioning what is happening and identifying where waste is created.

- A flowchart setting out each work process should include:
  - each stage in the process
  - raw materials and resources required at each stage
  - points where waste is/could be produced.

- Costs need to be clarified in order to produce a real picture of the actual costs of the waste itself, and the disposal of this waste.

- Future planning will enable ideas for waste reduction to be carefully prioritized.

- By defining the problem you will begin to consider cause and effect, i.e.
  - what is the actual cause of the waste that is being generated?
  - what is the real effect of the waste?

- An action plan for reducing waste will need to include:
  - the waste reduction issue
  - steps required to reduce the waste
  - who has responsibility for taking the necessary steps
  - timescales against which the steps will be taken
  - milestone points, review dates
  - methods of evaluation
  - desired outcome.

Performance checks

1 Quick quiz

Jot down the answers to the following questions on *Improving Efficiency*.

Question 1   What three kinds of transformations did we identify?

_____

_____

_____

Question 2   What **four** main types of resource did we identify?

_____

_____

_____

_____

Question 3   Define 'efficiency'.

_____

_____

Question 4   Explain the link between effectiveness and organizational objectives.

_____

_____

Question 5   Express, in your own words, the meaning of 'quality'.

_____

_____

Question 6   Explain, in your own words, the purpose of method study.

_____

_____

Question 7   List the **six** steps of method study.

_____

_____

_____

_____

_____

_____

Question 8   What methods of recording can be used during the recording stage of method study?

_____

_____

Question 9   What, in brief, is a string diagram used for?

_____

_____

Question 10   Give a definition of work measurement.

_____

_____

Question 11   What is continuous improvement and why is it an effective means of embedding change?

_____

_____

Question 12   What aspects of work can be affected by staff changes?

_____

Question 13   List three costs that a team leader needs to know and understand in relation to the use of resources.

_____

_____

_____

Question 14   What are the six stages of waste reduction?

_____

_____

_____

_____

_____

_____

Question 15   What are the three key features that a process flowchart needs to illustrate?

_____

_____

_____

Answers to these questions can be found on pages 107–8.

2 Workbook assessment

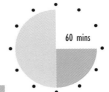

60 mins

Read the following case incident, and then deal with the questions which follow. Write your answers on a separate sheet of paper.

The management of the Sawbridge Timber and Frame Company would like to improve efficiency in the loading and transport of timber.

Jason White, one of their managers, is assigned to carry out an investigation of the problems in this area, and to propose a way forward. He is given authority to recommend any steps he believes are necessary, provided he is able to justify the expense.

After conducting a preliminary survey, Jason notes down two points as being the main problems resulting in inefficiency.

(a) Lorries are loaded by fork-lift truck. The process is slow, and there have been a number of incidents in which timber was damaged while being loaded. In one case, the cab of a lorry was crushed by falling timber, the driver fortunately not being in the cab at the time.

(b) During transport, average journey times seem to be longer than Jason would have expected.

In answering the following questions, you do not need to write more than a total of a page or so.

1 Suggest **four** possible reasons for the apparent slow and poor handling of timber during the loading process.

2 Assume that, in turn, each one of the four possible reasons listed in (1) is the actual problem. Explain briefly your ideas for finding a solution to this problem.

3 Suggest **three** possible reasons for the long journey times during transport.

4 Assume that, in turn, each one of the three possible reasons listed in question 3 is the actual problem. Briefly describe your ideas on potential solutions, setting out associated costs and benefits where possible.

3 Work-based assignment

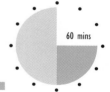

60 mins

Portfolio of evidence

S/NVQs B1.1, B1.2

The time guide for this assignment gives you an approximate idea of how long it is likely to take you to write up your findings. You will find you need to spend some additional time gathering information, talking to colleagues, and thinking about the assignment.

Your written response to this assignment may provide the basis of appropriate evidence for your S/NVQ portfolio. The assignment is also designed to help you to demonstrate your ability to support the efficient use of resources, by:

■ communicating
■ focusing on results
■ thinking and taking decisions.

What you have to do

In Session C, you should have begun work on a number of Activities designed to help you plan for the increased efficiency of your work team and work area. The relevant activities were:

People: Activity 21 on page 51, and 27 on page 59.

Workspace: Activity 22 on page 52, and 28 on page 60.

Equipment: Activity 23 on page 53, and 29 on page 61.

Materials: Activity 24 on page 54, and 30 on page 62.

Information: Activity 26 on page 56, and 32 on page 64.

Select one of the five resource items. Develop a plan to put in place changes that will result in demonstrable improvement in efficiency and effectiveness of work processes in your work area. This might include suggestions on potential areas of waste reduction, purchase or update of equipment, enhancing the skills and knowledge of staff.

Present your work in the form of a report addressed to your manager and any other individuals who will be part of the decision-making process if any of your changes are implemented. The content of the report should include:

- resource area selected, with reasons for your selection
- an account of the work you carried out during your investigations
- cost benefit analysis
- illustrations of the methods and techniques employed, for example the waste reduction six-stage process.

Reflect and review

1 Reflect and review

Now that you have completed your work on *Improving Efficiency*, let us review our workbook objectives.

■ You should be better able to recognize what efficiency means, in the context of your workplace.

Defining the word 'efficiency' is not difficult. The definition we used was: 'making the best use of resources, to achieve production of goods or services'. What is more relevant is how **you** view efficiency, now that you have finished the workbook, in relation to **your** resources and work processes.

Try to explain what you have learned, by answering the following questions.

■ What inefficiencies have I identified in the way I and my team operate?

_____

_____

_____

■ What are the effects of these inefficiencies on the organization as a whole?

_____

_____

_____

■ You will be better able to identify and use some method study techniques to help you improve efficiency and effectiveness.

You may not want to claim that you have become a method study expert as a result of reading this workbook, but you should have a better understanding of the techniques which might be available to you. All of these require the full commitment of higher management, and you would no doubt need to obtain approval before introducing any of them in your area.

■ Which of the techniques described in Session C do you feel would be useful in your work situation?

_____

_____

_____

■ How might you go about investigating the subject further?

_____

_____

_____

■ You will be better able to plan for the best use of resources assigned to you.

We spent a lot of time discussing resources. The Activities you tackled in Session C should have helped you to make plans to use the resources you have more efficiently.

As you should already have made some effort at developing resource plans, you might like now to consider the following two questions.

■ Are my resources adequate for my team's needs?

_____

_____

_____

■ What new approaches to resource efficiency can I think of?

_____

_____

_____

■ You will be better able to contribute effectively to the control of your organization's resources.

Efficiency involves controlling resources as well as planning for their best use. By reducing materials waste, for example, or using equipment to its full potential, you are controlling them, and saving your organization money in doing so.

■ Which types of resource do I feel I do **not** have under adequate control?

_____

_____

_____

■ What kinds of extra controls could I introduce to limit the wastage of resources?

_____

_____

_____

■ You will be better able to carry out a review of actual and potential waste generation points and take action to reduce waste accordingly.

Waste will be generated at different points of every work process and this waste will relate to each of the four resource areas – people, finance, capital and materials.

You might like to ask yourself the following questions.

■ Where can I see immediate areas for waste reduction within my area of work?

_____

_____

_____

■ What can I do to get my team involved in and committed to active waste reduction?

_____

_____

_____

■ You will be better able to play your part in helping to improve the efficiency of your work team and your organization.

This is the main purpose of the workbook, and all your efforts have been directed towards this aim.

■ What extra contribution might I make to the efficiency of my work team and/or my organization?

_____

_____

_____

■ How might I go about persuading my colleagues of the benefits of planning for improved efficiency?

_____

_____

_____

2 Action plan

Use this plan to further develop for yourself a course of action you want to take. Make a note in the left-hand column of the issues or problems you want to tackle, and then decide what you intend to do, and make a note in column 2.

The resources you need might include time, materials, information or money. You may need to negotiate for some of them, but they could be something easily acquired, like half an hour of somebody's time, or a chapter of a book. Put whatever you need in column 3. No plan means anything without a timescale, so put a realistic target completion date in column 4.

Finally, describe the outcome you want to achieve as a result of this plan, whether it is for your own benefit or advancement, or a more efficient way of doing things.

Desired outcomes				
1 Issues	2 Action	3 Resources	4 Target completion

Actual outcomes

3 Extensions

Extension 1

Book   Introduction to Operations Management
Author   John Naylor
Edition   2002
Publisher   Prentice Hall
ISBN   0 2736 5578 7

This book covers a number of the subjects of this workbook, including efficiency and effectiveness, transformation processes, work study, benchmarking, Total Quality Management, and continuous improvement. Particular chapters relevant to our subject are: Chapter 6 – Studying work; Chapter 8 – Facility layout: manufacture and isolated service; Chapter 9 – Facility layout: personal and self service.

As the Preface says: 'This book gives a comprehensive coverage of operations management for those who come to the subject for the first time.'

Extension 2

Book   Essentials of Production and Operations Management
Author   Ray Wild
Edition   Fifth edition, 2001
Publisher   The Continuum International Publishing Group
ISBN   0 8264 5254 X

This book covers all aspects of the operations and production management function, with a number of useful case studies to show how it inter-relates to the purchasing, supply, logistics and materials handling functions, in the use of systems like JIT, MRP and automated handling.

Extension 3

Book   Operations Management
Author   Howard Barnett
Edition   Second edition, 1996
Publisher   Palgrave Macmillan
ISBN   0 3336 6210 5

Operations Management provides a comprehensive introduction, clearly written and jargon-free, concentrating on examining the ways an organization turns its resources into goods or services. Some relevant chapters are Planning and Control, Managing the Costs, Managing the Processes, Managing

Performance 1: Getting the Methods Right, Managing Performance 2: Measuring Work Content, Managing Performance: Incentive Schemes, Managing Time and Managing Numbers 2: Statistical Process Control.

Extension 4   More information on waste management can be found on http://www. defra.gov.uk/environment/waste/index.htm

These extensions can be taken up via your ILM Centre. They will either have them or will arrange that you have access to them. However, it may be more convenient to check out the materials with your personnel or training people at work – they may well give you access. There are other good reasons for approaching your own people; for example, they will become aware of your interest and you can involve them in your development.

4 Answers to self-assessment questions

Self-assessment 1
page 23–4

1 The complete diagram is:

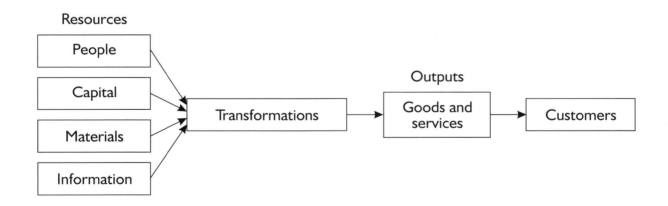

2   Compare your responses with the answer given below.

Transformation type	Sector			
	Manufacturing	Transport	Supply	Service
Improving	f	b	b	c, e
Caretaking	f	b	b	e
Transferring		a, b	a, b, d	

There may be some here which you disagree with.

(a) The regional electricity company transfers electricity from the National Grid to its customers. It is therefore in the transport and supply business. There is a case for putting it into the service sector, and you might say that it 'transports' electricity, by providing electricity cables.

(b) A water company has to purify (i.e. improve) and take care of water, and also transfer it to customers. It is in both the transport and supply business. Again, it might see itself as also providing a service.

(c) A hairdresser simply provides a hair-improving service.

(d) A hardware shop supplies goods to its customers, but does not improve them or take care of them (except in an incidental way). The shop may also pride itself on the good service it gives.

(e) A residential school improves and takes care of children, but does not supply, transport or manufacture them!

(f) A farm is a manufacturer, improving, and taking care of crops and farm animals and their products.

3   (a) EFFICIENCY means making the best use of RESOURCES, to achieve production of goods or SERVICES.

(b) Work organizations TRANSFORM resources (capital, materials and INFORMATION, with the help of PEOPLE) into goods and services, which are provided to their CUSTOMERS.

(c) QUALITY can be defined as all the FEATURES and characteristics of a product or service that affect its ability to SATISFY the needs of customers and USERS.

(d) For information to be valid and reliable it must be ACCURATE and complete.

4 Benefits to an organisation that result from control include:

- planning processes which are more likely to succeed
- achievement of objectives
- identification and use of resources which are of the correct quality and quantity
- ability to take appropriate corrective action – a less reactive, more proactive response to problems
- improved forecasting and estimating
- thorough assessment of performance, enabling constructive feedback and improved staff performance overall.

**Self-assessment 2
pages 46–7**

1 The overall productivity is:

$$\frac{\text{output}}{\text{input}} = \frac{4500}{2500} = 1.8$$

The output per head is:

$$\frac{£4500}{5} = £900$$

2 (a) QUANTITATIVE is the term used when costs are described in numerical terms or units. QUALITATIVE is the term used when costs are set out in broad descriptive or less tangible terms.
(b) To justify the purchase of a new piece of equipment, or any form of change, it is generally accepted that the total BENEFITS will exceed the total costs.
(c) In undertaking any form of WORK MEASUREMENT the business will be seeking to identify and introduce methods for improving process efficiency.
(d) In the second stage of time study you will break down the job into phases called ELEMENTS.

3 The correct diagram is:

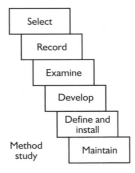

4 The four main areas of consideration in method study are financial, technical, human and environmental.

5 Factors that affect managers in their own working area in relation to human resource planning include:

- numbers of staff needed to carry out current work requirements
- skills and knowledge levels required to carry out these work requirements, possibly in the form of job specifications for each role within the department or team
- potential changes to work requirements, based on information gathered
- organizational, departmental and team objectives
- number and types of staff required to fulfil these objectives.

Self-assessment 3 pages 65–6

1 (a) If you get your team fully MOTIVATED and working towards the right OBJECTIVES, efficiency and effectiveness will follow almost automatically.
  (b) A COACH is someone who aims to get the best out of people: the best EFFORTS, the best ACHIEVEMENTS, the best IDEAS.
  (c) It is the TEAM who must get the job done, and it is the LEADER's role to provide them with the means to do it: to EMPOWER them.
  (d) Badly used workspace can result in CONGESTION, ACCIDENTS, inefficient COMMUNICATIONS, excessive ENERGY costs or low PRODUCTION.

2 Ways to save energy in an office could include:

- switching off lights and heating when they aren't needed
- switching off equipment when it isn't needed
- keeping doors and windows closed when heating is on
- getting the building properly insulated.

3 Some suggestions are:

- keep better records of expenditure, ensuring they are complete, accurate and accessible
- ensure you monitor and maintain resources such as equipment and materials in accordance with organizational requirements
- keep your team members informed of their individual responsibilities for the control of resources.

4 Examples of costs associated with the use of resources include:

- costs of running an item of equipment
- costs of an item of equipment lying idle
- cost of running a faulty, poorly maintained item of equipment
- costs of staff
- costs of replacing staff
- costs of producing items, and the marginal costs of producing just one more item than is required.

**Self-assessment 4
pages 86–7**

1 (a) Most organizations rarely calculate the true MONETARY cost of waste.

(b) All CONTRIBUTORY factors within a work process need to be taken into account when calculating the cost of waste.

(c) A waste reduction AWARENESS CAMPAIGN can usefully kick-start awareness raising. Ongoing reminders of the IMPORTANCE of waste reduction will be essential to keeping the process alive within the business.

(d) A GOOD AND CLEAR definition of the waste reduction issue will provide a useful starting point for arriving at practical SOLUTIONS.

2 The six stages in managing waste reduction are:

1 Awareness raising
2 Process analysis
3 Clarifying costs
4 Future planning
5 Defining the problem and identifying solutions
6 Taking action.

3 Key factors in ensuring that waste reduction action plans are implemented include:

- sound definition of the waste reduction issue, which everyone concerned can understand and relate to
- a series of realistic steps that will result in waste reduction
- allocation of responsibility for different steps needs to be given to those who are able to take the necessary action
- ensuring that those with allocated responsibility have the relevant authority and access to the necessary resources
- review dates are adhered to
- evaluation methods suit the types of action required
- the desired outcome is set in terms which are measurable.

5 Answers to activities

**Activity 3
on page 7**

You may have noted as people your own work team, or included other departments such as sales, accounts, shop staff, operators, and so on.

Capital could be the building you work in, the equipment you use in your job, the budgets you work to, or the ground you stand on.

The materials you listed will depend on the kind of work you do; they might be made from paper, metal, plastic, ceramics, etc. You may have included gas, electricity or oil as energy consumed.

Information could be in the form of specifications, job descriptions, formulations, reports, and so on.

Activity 6
on page 12

Other examples of inefficiency might include:

- using unskilled labour, which may result in need for reworking and a return to the transformation stage
- poor transformation processes, which result in waste and low quality outputs.

Other examples of ineffectiveness might include:

- not agreeing what the objectives are or having no clear objectives to aim for – all parts of the model would be adversely affected
- too many resources being used to return minimal profit through low sales.

Activity 15
on page 32

The costs can be classified as follows:

1 In the investigation of possible suppliers, calls are **quantitative**, travel is **quantitative**, time is **qualitative**.

2 The actual purchase (or lease if this is an option) is **quantitative**

3 The installation and commissioning of the equipment is **quantitative**.

4 The delivery and location on-site is **quantitative** and **qualitative.**

5 Time spent training staff on how to use is **quantitative** and **qualitative.**

6 Running of existing equipment during phasing-in stage – duplicate costs are **quantitative.**

7 In regard to down time if old equipment is to be removed before installation of new, loss of profit is **quantitative**, loss of time is **qualitative.**

8 Staff down time while waiting for installation loss of profit is **quantitative**, loss of time is **qualitative.**

9 The potential opportunity costs are both all the **quantitative** costs listed above and all the **qualitative** costs, plus any other relevant factors.

6 Answers to the quick quiz

Answer 1   The three transformation types were improving, caretaking and transferring.

Answer 2   The four resource types were people, capital, materials and information.

Answer 3   We defined efficiency as 'making the best use of resources, to achieve production of goods and services'.

Answer 4   One way of expressing this relationship is to say that, to be effective, an organization, individual or group has to achieve agreed objectives.

Answer 5   Quality can be defined as all the features and characteristics of a product or service which affect its ability to satisfy the needs of customers and users.

Answer 6   Method study can be defined as: 'Systematically recording the way work is done, followed by analysis and development of the new methods, with the aim of doing the work better.'

Answer 7   We listed the steps of method study as: select, record, examine, develop, define and install, and maintain.

Answer 8   The recording methods that can be used are flow process diagrams, string diagrams and multiple activity charts.

Answer 9   A string diagram is used to determine the distance travelled by a person (or materials, equipment or information).

Answer 10   Work measurement is defined as the use of techniques to establish how long it takes a qualified worker to do a specified job to a defined level of performance.

Answer 11   In continuous improvement staff make suggestions on potential improvements that can be made. Continuous improvement is recognised as a more effective means of embedding change where suggestions for improvement have been made by those who are most affected by this change.

Answer 12   The aspects of work affected by staff changes are productivity and quality.

Answer 13   Costs that a manager needs to know and understand in relation to the use of resources include:

- the costs of running an item of equipment
- the costs of an item of equipment lying idle
- the cost of running a faulty, poorly maintained item of equipment
- the costs of staff
- the costs of replacing staff
- the costs of producing items, and the marginal costs of producing just one more item than is required.

Answer 14   The six stages of waste reduction are:

1   Awareness raising.
2   Process analysis.
3   Clarifying costs.
4   Future planning.
5   Defining the problem and identifying solutions.
6   Taking action.

Answer 15   The three key features that a process flowchart needs to illustrate are:

1   Each stage in the process.
2   Raw materials and resources required at each stage.
3   Points where waste is/could be produced.

7 Certificate

Completion of this certificate by an authorized person shows that you have worked through all the parts of this workbook and satisfactorily completed the assessments. The certificate provides a record of what you have done that may be used for exemptions or as evidence of prior learning against other nationally certificated qualifications.

Pergamon Flexible Learning and ILM are always keen to refine and improve their products. One of the key sources of information to help this process are people who have just used the product. If you have any information or views, good or bad, please pass these on.

INSTITUTE OF LEADERSHIP & MANAGEMENT

SUPERSERIES

Improving Efficiency

....

has satisfactorily completed this workbook

Name of signatory ....

Position ....

Signature ....

Date ....

Official stamp

Fourth Edition

INSTITUTE OF LEADERSHIP & MANAGEMENT
SUPERSERIES
FOURTH EDITION

To order – phone us direct for prices and availability details
(please quote ISBNs when ordering) on 01865 888190